BARRY

ITS RAILWAY & PORT

BEFORE & **AFTER** WOODHAM'S SCRAPYARD

JOHN HODGE

FRONT COVER: On Summer Sundays and Bank Holidays an excursion ran from the Sirhowy Valley to Barry Island, dating back to the early years of the century. In the 1950s, the down train arrived around midday and returned at 7.35pm, hauled by a former London & North Western 0-8-0 which turned on the Dock at Barry. Here we see Tredegar's 49064 with the return train on 26th May 1958, the last year of former LNW haulage, passing Cadoxton Low Level Signal Box, before joining the former Barry Main Line via Wenvoe.

TITLE PAGE: An everyday scene at No. 1 Dock as a small coaster awaits loading at No. 1 Tip where a vessel is currently loading. The view is from the point at which the passenger ferry operated carrying the public across the Dock to near the C.H. Bailey Dry Dock from where they could walk to either Jackson's Bay or Barry Island. The ferry was first provided for workmen but was later made available to the public and was very well used.

BACK COVER: A panoramic view from Ship Hill Bridge of the modern scene at Barry station as a Pacer leaves with the 10.5am to Bridgend in October 2016. M.J. Back.

BARRY

ITS RAILWAY & PORT

BEFORE & **AFTER** WOODHAM'S SCRAPYARD

JOHN HODGE

PEN & SWORD
TRANSPORT

First published in Great Britain in 2018 by
Pen & Sword Transport

An imprint of
Pen & Sword Books Ltd
Yorkshire - Philadelphia

ISBN 978 1 52672 3 833

A CIP catalogue record for this book is available from the British Library

Typeset in Palatino
Typeset by Pen & Sword Books Ltd

Printed and bound in India by Replika Press Pvt. Ltd.

Pen & Sword Books Ltd incorporates the Imprints of Aviation, Atlas,
Family History, Fiction, Maritime, Military, Discovery, Politics, History,
Archaeology, Select, Wharncliffe Local History, Wharncliffe True Crime,
Military Classics, Wharncliffe Transport, Leo Cooper, The Praetorian Press,
Remember When, Seaforth Publishing and Frontline Publishing.

For a complete list of Pen & Sword titles please contact

PEN & SWORD BOOKS LTD
47 Church Street, Barnsley, South Yorkshire, S70 2AS, England
E-mail: enquiries@pen-and-sword.co.uk
Website: www.pen-and-sword.co.uk

Or
PEN AND SWORD BOOKS
1950 Lawrence Rd, Havertown, PA 19083, USA
E-mail: Uspen-and-sword@casematepublishers.com
Website: www.penandswordbooks.com

CONTENTS

DEDICATION

I DEDICATE THIS book to those who educated me at Barry Grammar School which I attended from 1948 to 1956. What a wonderful array of highly professional masters there were during that period and before. My main dealings were with the following to whom I am ever grateful for their expertise: Griffith Caradoc Hughes (French); Teifion Phillips (History); Percy Fisher (English); Eric Jones (Maths); Gwyn Thomas (Spanish); Bryn Ashton (Latin); Digby Lloyd (Physics); Sidney Perkins (Chemistry) and many others, each of whom had his personal nickname. Unfortunately, the history curriculum contained no reference to local history, so when I left I knew nothing about the development of the Docks from 1884, or the Barry Railway, a significant omission to my education which I have had to rectify since.

ACKNOWLEDGEMENTS

IN MY RESEARCH, I have used Martin J. Beckett's excellent little book *The Barry Story*, published in 1982, mostly for details of the number of engines bought for scrapping by Woodhams and their ultimate fate.

PREFACE

SOME READERS WILL only have heard of Barry in connection with the Scrapyard run by Dai Woodham during the 1960s and '70s, from which most of the engines were bought and restored to run on our heritage railways. But the railways and docks at Barry have a complete history all of their own which had achieved huge importance and fascination well before the Scrapyard ever existed. This book sets out to describe the Docks and Railway development and activities before and after the Scrapyard years with short sections on each aspect.

I lived at Barry for twenty-eight years from 1942 to 1970 and, though only young, saw some of the wartime activity at the Docks. Much of the comment relative to this period stems from my own experience and recollection. Almost all the photographs are from my own collection, both during the above period and on my visits since, but I have also used images by J.G. Hubback, whose collection I acquired in the late 1950s, some modern images by my friend Michael J. (Mike) Back of Efail Isaf, plus a few images bought in. Where no credit appears, these are photos taken by me or from my own collection.

INTRODUCTION

MY FAMILY MOVED to Barry from Crosskeys, in the Western Valley, in 1942, when I was coming up to the ripe old age of four, and we soon moved to a house in Dock View Road, near the Sea View Labour Club, which overlooked a fantastic panorama of transport. Across the road, allotments ran from one end of the road to the other, about six to ten feet below road level as the road climbed and fell. Below this was a steep bank about twenty to thirty feet down, below which was the main line from Barry Docks to Cadoxton, and a few feet below this was the line into the Docks from Cadoxton Low Level, four tracks, two into the Old (No. 1) Dock, and two into the New (No. 2) Dock, both entering tunnels right in front of our house. Above the tunnels and on the same level as the main line was Barry Docks Storage Sidings, where thousands of coal wagons, loaded and empty, were marshalled for shipment and return empty to the collieries. Some general freight was also marshalled in these sidings. Beyond the marshalling yard were the tracks leading to the coal hoists where coal wagons were tipped into the ships berthed at the hoists on the north side of No. 2 Dock.

On the south side of the Dock was Rank's Flour Mill, where incoming ships would unload their cargo for processing and later at the south-west end of the Dock was the berth for the Geest Banana Traffic which became the main traffic, other than coal, from the mid-1950s until the company departed for Southampton in the mid-1960s. On the north side of the dock were ten coal hoists or tips, where

The view from our house in Dock View Road looking across the Railway and Dock out to the Bristol Channel. A 350HP diesel shunter brings loaded banana wagons from No. 2 Dock to Cadoxton Low Level from where main line trains started in the early 1960s. The vessel from which the bananas were discharged can be seen in the top right of the picture.

Following the demise of shipment coal traffic through Barry, the closure of Barry Goods and the end of the scrapping programme, Barry Docks Storage Sidings were recovered and a large engineering project was created to open up the tunnels serving the Dock lines, by now reduced to a single line serving No. 2 Dock. The tunnels were then bridged again and converted into a road. This view from our bedroom window shows the work in progress with a Class 56 diesel on the evening chemical train to Blackpool in the 1990s. The line in the foreground is the down main line.

coal wagons were unloaded into the ships berthed below them, five tips being removed in the late 1950s to be replaced by high capacity cranes for the import of bulk cargoes. Beyond the docks lay the Bristol Channel where vessels for Barry Docks would lie at anchor in Barry Roads until their tidal time arrived for entry, and pilot boats and tugs would ply between them to arrange their passage into the docks, if this was necessary. In the days after the war, the public could walk freely through the docks, and there was even a ferry service across No. 1 Dock to take passengers from just below the Dock Offices on the north side across to the bottom of Battery Hill, near the C.H. Bailey Dry Dock, on the south side from where they could walk either to Jackson's Bay or to Barry Island.

I would spend hours as a young lad looking through the railings which separated the allotments from the road, at the never-ending shunting of coal wagons, loaded and empty, at the trains passing along the main line and at the movement of vessels in the Docks and out

in the Channel. I especially remember a main line special train with a Hall Class engine coming out of No. 2 Dock Tunnel loaded with soldiers returning from the war as I watched through the railings, with many leaning out of the windows and waving to the little lad then aged about seven who was watching this rare event. Little wonder my interest and employment in later life was to be solely in the field of transport.

I soon began taking photographs of ships in the Docks and of the railways and would cycle around the Docks to record various subjects and views. In 1953, I met the Shedmaster from Barry Engine Shed, Ernie Breakspear, and he invited me to go down to the shed on a Sunday morning in March to see a Swansea Docks Shunter No. 1151 which had arrived for works. I went there every Sunday morning until 1961. I soon also met the Works Foreman, a Mr. Elias, who asked me if I was interested in his records of all the engines that had previously been repaired at the works. I borrowed his notebooks going back to 1937 and my archive now contains details of all the engines which passed through Barry Works from 1937 until closure in 1959.

On summer weekends and Bank Holidays, excursions to Barry Island were the main feature of interest, especially those emanating from main line origins, whose main line tender engine had to return light to Canton to be turned and serviced. My all-time favourite was seeing Star No. 4051 Princess Helena of Worcester, ex-works on an excursion from Worcester. There were excursions from all the Cardiff and Newport Valleys, including from the Sirhowy Valley with an ex-LNW 0-8-0. These excursions had started life as originating at Abergavenny, running along the MT&A, and getting so full that another train had to be started at Brynmawr. Up to five such trains had been necessary in the earlier years of the century, but in my day, it was one excursion first from Brynmawr, then Nantybwch, though sometimes with a charter conveying a party from Holly Bush.

Since 1948, I had spent many hours at Cardiff General Station, and had got to know the Assistant Station Master Fred Jones quite well. In 1960, he was appointed Station Master Barry and I used to go over to Barry Island station to see him in the West Box from where I took many excellent photographs of returning excursions from positions of advantage. After I began working in the Cardiff District Train Office in 1961, I used to go with him to Barry Signal Box on winter days when there were main line diversions due to engineering work on the main line.

Through my friendship with Ernie Breakspear, I got an introduction to Canton Shed office, and the Shedmaster, W.W. (Bill) Wagstaff (who used to be a shed foreman at Barry), in the mid-1950s to study the engine diagrams, and used to go there regularly to study the engine records and take photographs, with the blessing of the shed foremen Charlie Hewlett and Ivor Hockey, both of whom I got to know very well.

The start of the Woodham era for me was seeing long rakes of unfitted vans and wagons lined up in the sidings opposite our house from the late 1950s, when I was at University in Cardiff. Starting work from University in September 1961 in the Cardiff District Train Office, I worked inter alia on a subject I already knew very well, the Summer excursion traffic to Barry Island, and in 1963 produced the first all DMU bank holiday working, which worked very well. My interest in the Woodham activity included the types of wagons and brakevans that were brought in for scrap, as well as on the engines. I saw the first engines sent to Barry for scrapping, which were four 53XXs when Woodham did in fact do some scrapping of engines, a practice he ceased to concentrate on wagons and coaches, to the benefit of the steam engines which he later sold off to the preservationists. I saw many of the engines that were the most famous of the Barry scrapyard era, the two Kings 6023 and 6024 and 71000 which stood right outside our house in Dock View Road on the railway sidings for several days until moved onto the Docks, then being rescued for preservation.

I moved away from Barry in 1970 to take a position at the WR HQ Offices at Paddington, married in 1971 and moved to Haywards Heath in West Sussex, becoming a Brighton line commuter for thirty years until retirement in 1992. Recollections of my teenage years at Barry remain vivid in my memory and I hope will bring back similar memories to readers while also introducing what the railway in Barry was like in the pre-Woodham scrapyard days. The sections in this book must of needs be short in order to include all the activities concerned with the Barry scene, and I have also included the railway position as it is today so readers can identify with what they can still see happening currently.

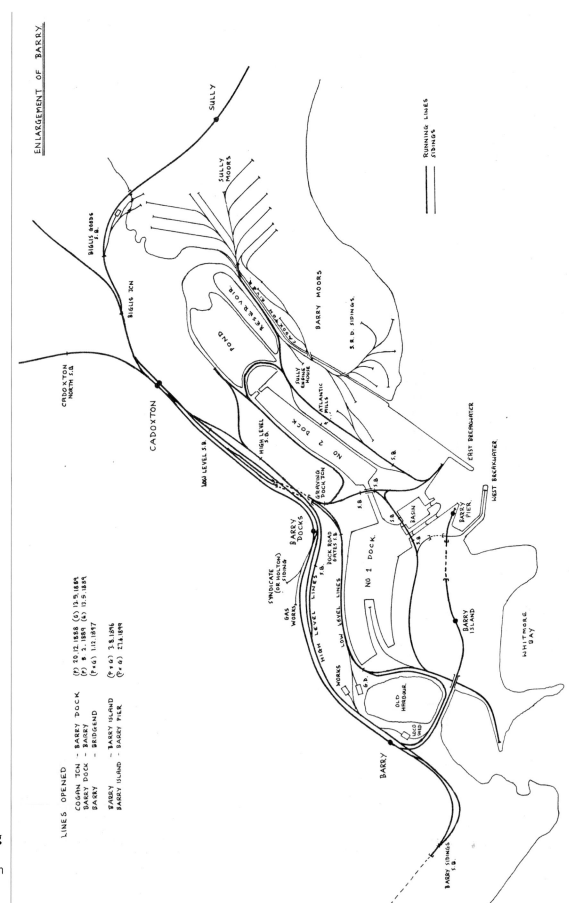

An overall drawing of the Railway and Docks at Barry when all fully operative.
Courtesy R.A. Cooke

CHAPTER 1

THE BARRY RAILWAY

THE ACT TO create a new Dock and Railway at Barry was accepted by Parliament in 1884, having been opposed and rejected in 1883. The case for a new Dock at Barry hinged on the inability of Cardiff Docks and the Taff Vale Railway to cope with the ever-increasing volume of coal shipment traffic emanating from the Rhondda and Rhymney Valleys, and the heavy delays in train working. The work on building a new line from Barry to Trehafod, and a branch to Cogan, both then joining with the Taff Vale lines, was immediately put in hand under the Barry Dock & Railway Co. with David Davies MP (1818-90) as Chairman and Archibald Hood (1823-1902), who took over as Chairman when Davies died. The engineers responsible were John Wolfe Barry, James W. Szlumper and T.A. Walker.

With little in the way of engineering problems other than the need for tunnels at Wenvoe, Pontypridd and a short one approaching Cogan, the main line from Barry to Hafod Junction was ready for inspection by November 1888, while the first passenger train to run between Barry Dock and Cogan did so in December 1888. In February 1889, the passenger service was extended west from Barry Dock to Barry. The main line to Hafod Junction was opened for goods traffic in May 1889 with a connection from Tynycaeau Junction to St. Fagans into the GWR line. However, when the company extended into the Rhymney Valley in the new century, heavy expenditure was incurred on three large viaducts, at Walnut Tree (Taffs Well), at Llanbradach and at Penyrheol.

Construction of the Dock was complete by June 1889 with the first water let in on the 29th. The ceremonial opening of the Dock took place on 18 July 1889, when the first coal trains began to run between Trehafod, Treforest and Barry. The need to attract coal traffic from the Tondu Valleys in the west was recognised by the creation of the Vale of Glamorgan Railway Co. in August 1889, the line opening in December 1897.

In August 1891, the company changed its name to the Barry Railway Co. and the passenger service was extended from Cogan to Cardiff Riverside in August 1893 with an extension to Clarence Road in April 1894.

A passenger service began between Barry, Pontypridd (Graig) and Porth in March 1896, with a new branch to Barry Island in August 1896. June 1897 saw the extension of the passenger service to run from Pontypridd (Graig) to Cardiff via St.Fagans. Disaster befell the Vale of Glamorgan line just over a month after opening when subsidence affected a pier of the 376-yard Porthkerry Viaduct which closed the line until a loop line could be built from Porthkerry to east of Rhoose, passengers being conveyed in horse-drawn brakes, and coal trains diverted while the viaduct was repaired. The loop line was completed and opened on 25 April 1898 and carried all traffic, coal and passengers, until the viaduct could be satisfactorily repaired, this being achieved by 8 January 1900 when it was re-opened for coal and goods traffic, passenger traffic resuming on 9 April.

The success of Barry Dock was overwhelming and an extension was built opening in 1898, known as the No. 2 or New Dock, the original becoming No. 1

or the Old Dock. On 27 July 1899, the line was extended from Barry Island through a tunnel to Barry Pier from where steamer services could be accessed for pleasure trips across the Bristol Channel to Weston, Minehead and Ilfracombe. From August 1904, the Barry Co. ran its own steamers under the Barry Railway (Steam Vessels) Act but this was short-lived and they soon sold out to P.& A. Campbell who operated such services until the 1960s.

In their plans to access collieries in the Rhymney Valley, a new line was opened from Tynycaeau Junction (between Wenvoe and Creigiau) to Penrhos Junction in August 1901. This line crossed the Taff on the newly built Walnut Tree Viaduct at Taffs Well and then ran through the newly built Walnut Tree Tunnel, 490 yards long. As part of a massive new network of access lines, the Barry had then built viaducts at Llanbradach and Penyrheol to access the main Rhymney Valley and the Senghenydd and Windsor Colliery line. In 1905, they finally achieved access to the Brecon & Merthyr line at Barry Junction, later Duffryn Isaf Junction. This was the last of their expansionist plans.

As might be expected, the Barry Company tried to undercut the Taff Vale coal rates to their new Dock, but in this they were fiercely resisted and by an Act of Parliament coal rates from the valley collieries to either Cardiff or Barry were fixed as the same, no matter by which line, to Cardiff, Penarth or Barry Docks. By the end of the first decade of the new century, Barry Docks had overtaken the mighty Cardiff Docks in coal shipment tonnage and became the greatest coal shipment port in the world at that time. Following the end of the 1914-18 War, the Barry Company, like the other private companies, was in financial difficulties and the level of coal shipment fell as ships began using oil instead of coal. In 1922, the Barry Company joined the rest of the local South Wales railways in being amalgamated into the Great Western Railway.

Map of extent of the Barry Railway

The A Class
0-6-0T were the first engines used on the Barry Railway from 1889, for both passenger and coal services. There were five engines in the class built by Sharp Stewart in November 1888, the last surviving to May 1932. No. 1 is here seen at Barry Goods. Charles Farmer/ Barry Railway/Austin Smith Collection.

The B Class 0-6-2T very quickly followed the A and was very similar other than in the extension to carry a larger coal bunker with a trailing wheel. Twenty-five of the class were built between December 1888 and February 1890 by Sharp Stewart, the last surviving to October 1949. No. 32 is seen here probably at Barry Shed. Charles Farmer/Barry Railway/Austin Smith Collection.

The B1 Class 0-6-2T was a modified B Class with larger side tanks to enable them to carry sufficient water to avoid stopping to refill en route between Cadoxton and Trehafod. Forty-two of the class were built and until the arrival of more powerful engines, they worked the coal services between the Rhondda and Cadoxton Yard. Some B and B1s were allocated to Hafod and Coity while these depots remained open and the GWR allocated some to other local depots, especially Radyr. Both the B and B1s were demoted to tripping and shunting, mostly around Barry and Radyr following the Grouping, the last surviving until April 1951. Here No. 112 is seen at Cadoxton Yard. Charles Farmer/ Barry Railway/Austin Smith Collection.

The C Class 2-4-0T consisted of 4 engines by Sharp Stewart, two of which were sold to the Port Talbot Railway. They were the first purely passenger engines and worked the Barry to Cogan service, being converted in 1898 to 2-4-2T in Barry Works. They were eclipsed by the new J Class after which they performed secondary passenger duties, both being withdrawn by May 1928. Here GWR 1322 is seen at Barry Shed. W. Beckerlegge/Author's Collection.

The D Class 0-8-0, introduced between 1886-88, was the first of this wheel arrangement in the country and the only tender engines on the Barry Railway. They were bought from Sharp Stewart as part of a failed order to the Swedish & Norwegian Railway. Initially, they worked only on movement of shipment coal from Cadoxton to the tips. From 1909, they were used on workings to the collieries, but returned to local duties after the Grouping and were withdrawn between the end of 1927 and 1930. No. 93 is seen here at Cadoxton Yard. Charles Farmer/Barry Railway/Austin Smith Collection.

The E Class 0-6-0T, five engines built by Hudswell Clarke between August 1889 and March 1891, were used for light work around the dock where access was restricted, especially the lighthouse branch through a very narrow tunnel. In 1909, No. 33 was converted to an 0-4-2T to work an auto set working between Barry and Llantwit Major, the auto working later being discontinued. Only two remained at Barry (Nos. 783/4), the others disposed of to Cathays, Cardiff East Dock and Reading Signals before ending their days at collieries. No. 33 is here seen outside Barry Works. Charles Farmer/Barry Railway/Austin Smith Collection.

No. 33, as an 0-4-2T, with the auto set at Barry station. Author's Collection.

The F Class saddle tank 0-6-0T consisting of twenty-eight engines was introduced from March 1900 to May 1905, the last one withdrawn in January 1937. Mainly used for shunting at Barry Dock Storage Sidings, other yards around Barry and on the Docks, they were popular with the GWR and were allocated to Cardiff East Dock, Cathays, Canton, Pill, Neath and Duffryn Yard after the Grouping, only eight remaining at Barry. Some were converted to pannier tanks and were the forerunners of the 67XX series of dock shunters in South Wales. Several ended their days at collieries. Here we see No. 72 in Cadoxton Yard. Charles Farmer/Barry Railway/Austin Smith Collection.

The G Class 0-4-4T were a passenger class introduced from August 1892 to March 1895, built by the Vulcan Foundry and Sharp Stewart, They were initially used on the Cogan service, then on to Cardiff, but after the introduction of the J Class in 1898, they were switched to the Pontypridd line where they worked to/from Barry and Cardiff. They were all withdrawn between May 1925 and April 1929. No. 69 is seen alongside the shed wall at Barry. Author's Collection.

The H Class 0-8-2T, 7 engines built by Sharp Stewart in 1896, were originally intended for the Vale of Glamorgan line working, and until that line was completed, they were used on the line to Trehafod. As the B1 Class was capable of working this service, the H Class was employed on Cadoxton Yard to Barry Dock working when they took over 100 loaded wagons on the short journey. Introduction of the 4200 and 5600 Class at Barry in the 1920s rendered the class surplus and they were all withdrawn by August 1930. No. 83 is seen here at Cadoxton Yard. Charles Farmer/Barry Railway/Austin Smith Collection.

The J Class 2-4-2T, 11 engines built between May 1898 and June 1899 by Hudswell Clarke and Sharp Stewart, were the star passenger engines of the company and worked the services to Cardiff and Bridgend. Like the G Class, they were always maintained in prime condition with brasswork all highly polished. Four of the class were withdrawn in 1926, four in 1928 and the final three in 1930. Here No. 89 stands alongside the shed wall.
Author's Collection.

The K Class 0-6-2T of five engines were built by the Cooke Loco. & Machine Co. of New Jersey, and though the Barry were seeking a design similar to the B1, they had to accept certain features of American design. The engines were heavy on coal consumption and were withdrawn from main line mineral working on that account, being employed on banking and with the several others on loaded and empty movement from and to Cadoxton Yard. All were withdrawn between 1927 and 1932. Here No. 121 is seen in Cadoxton Yard. Charles Farmer/Barry Railway/Austin Smith Collection.

The L Class 0-6-4T was the last design of the Barry Railway in 1914 with ten engines built by Hawthorn, Leslie. With a tractive effort of almost 25k lbs., they were very powerful on coal services but had a propensity to derail. Being non-standard to the GWR, they were all withdrawn in October 1926, though they could have easily been rebuilt. Here, No. 143 as GWR 1351 is seen at Barry Shed.

L Class No. 144 in a Barry Railway picture at Cadoxton Yard with a train of empties bound for a colliery.

A Sunday view of the shed yard probably in the early years of the Grouping as there are GWR engines in the distance.

An example of a Barry Railway 20ton Brakevan No.67

CHAPTER 2
BARRY DOCKS

BARRY OWES ITS very existence to the development of the Docks and Railway to serve them. In the decade before the building of the Docks, there were only about a hundred people resident in the locality of Barry, mostly in the areas of Merthyr Dyfan and Cadoxton where they were farmers and agricultural workers, craftsmen and traders. Before the problems of congestion at Cardiff Docks of the 1880s, which led to the ultimate development of Barry Docks, a previous attempt had been made to develop a dock at Barry. John Thomas, a retired farmer from Barry Island, produced a plan for a coastal railway out of the new South Wales Railway to run from Pencoed through Cowbridge, Aberthaw and Barry and link with the new Taff Vale Railway at Cogan, with a new dock at Barry for the export of coal and limestone and the import of hay and foodstuffs for the Valleys.

His plan attracted considerable attention in the area and a local railway engineer, H. Voss, saw the potential both of carrying coal by this route to the new Penarth Docks and the Bute Docks at Cardiff, but also of building a large dock at Barry. He approached the Jenners of Wenvoe Castle and together they drew up a plan for a dock and a railway linking into the Taff Vale railway at Cogan, securing a series of Acts for the construction and for a narrow gauge railway. In 1866, Jenner secured the Barry Harbour Act which authorised a 600 yard quay to be built from where the Buttrills Brook joined the sea near the north-west end of the eventual No. 1 Dock, plus the deepening of the Cadoxton River which joined the sea at Cold Knap, which would allow for large ships to berth at the quay. The Act allowed for the setting up of a Barry Railway Company and a Barry

Harbour Company.

The plans were never realised as they failed to attract the necessary support of the coal owners, who preferred to continue to operate at Cardiff Docks. Though Jenner continued to maintain an interest, the act for the building of the new Bute Dock at Cardiff of 1874 killed off his plans for Barry, but others in the area still saw the potential of a coastal railway from Penarth through Sully to Cadoxton, and this was approved by the Penarth Extension Railway Act of the Taff Vale Railway in 1876, the line opening in February 1878, bringing population and trade to swell the agricultural nature of the village of Cadoxton.

The new Bute Dock at Cardiff was victim of its own success and was quite unable to keep pace with the developing Rhondda Valley coal mines. There were far too many trains trying to run each day south of Pontypridd to Cardiff Docks and it was taking best part of a day for them to complete a journey from the top of the Rhondda to Cardiff Docks, with heavy dock dues to be paid to the Bute family for use of their new facilities. There was mounting concern at the position and a group of Rhondda valley coal owners, led by Archibald Hood of the Glamorgan Coal Co. and John Cory who was establishing a network of coal bunkering depots around the world. They prevailed upon David Davies of the Ocean Coal Co. to lead the venture as he had better standing as a Member of Parliament to get a scheme authorised, especially with his previous background in railway construction. They sought to build a new dock at Barry to which they would channel their Rhondda Valley coal on their own railway, thus bypassing the Taff Vale Railway, giving them full control both in terms of dock shipment and rail

The statue of David Davies outside the former Barry Docks and Railway Offices.

The statue of Archibald Hood at Llwynypia.

transport. A first proposal of 1883 failed but this was renewed in 1884 and was successful, an act of Parliament for a new railway and dock being passed in August of that year, with the first sod being cut at Castleland Point on 14 November 1884. Principal Engineer was John Wolfe Barry (whose father Charles Barry was engineer for the Tower Bridge and Surrey Commercial Docks). He was assisted by Thomas Forster Brown and Henry Marc Brunel (son of Isambard Kingdom Brunel) with John Robinson as Resident Engineer, the works to be built by T.A. Walker who had recently completed the Severn Tunnel. This formidable team of engineers not only built the dock and railway but also residential and trading properties as workers and shopkeepers flooded into the area as was common when such large enterprises were begun.

Before construction of the dock could begin, an area of some 200 acres needed to be made clear and safe from the sea requiring three dams to be constructed between the sea at Barry Island and the mainland. The middle dam divided the dock in half, a second dammed the encroaching sea from the west (at what was later known as the Old Harbour) and a third from the east, so that the dock construction site was completely cut off from the sea. The dams against the sea were not without problems in their constriction as initially they sank into the mud which was up to 40ft deep and were carried away by the tide; but eventually they fulfilled their purpose. Timber structures had to be erected to carry loaded trucks of waste from excavations elsewhere to be tipped to form the dams. It was July 1885 before the damming was complete, with sluice pipes laid to pump away water which had still succeeded in breaking through. Work at low tide was furious to get as much additional material banked up as possible before the tide turned. The final act was to drop shutters between horizontal timber structures to seal off the area, backed up by as much stone and earth as possible from trucks brought in from elsewhere on the site. Even so, a sluice pipe 40in in diameter was still necessary to clear the excess water, this having to be closed off at high tide. A Cornish engine pump originally from the Severn Tunnel works, pumped 120,000 gallons per hour from the dock site. The western dam became the railway bank and the road known as the Causeway between Barry and Barry Island.

Explosives were used to bring down embankments etc. and the spoil was removed and loaded to railway trucks by steam shovels. Obviously, an initial engineering work was to create sufficient flat areas between the island and the mainland on which to lay railway tracks on which engines and wagons could be run safely. The degree to which this was necessary can be appreciated by studying the incline of Battery Hill from the Marine down to the finished dock level. The eastern dam was completed in March 1886 and the area faced with brickwork in cement mortar.

In addition to the dock itself, holding sidings and link sidings between these and the coal hoists had to be built, again involved large scale land flattening with much demolition being involved

A trial with a Barry Railway Co. wagon on one of the coal hoists being erected in 1889. National Museum of Wales.

to achieve this over the complete area between the present Barry, Barry Docks and Cadoxton which needed to be left completely flat. Two separate large areas of land were laid out as holding sidings for inwards loaded and outward empty coal wagons, at Cadoxton and between Cadoxton, Barry Dock and Barry, the centre section between Cadoxton and Barry Docks station being added after the construction of No. 2 Dock in 1898.

Barry Dock nearing completion in 1889.

Filling the Dock in 1889.

The opening of Barry Dock in July 1889 with the *SS Arno*, the first ship to enter, on the left.

As construction proceeded, a significant change was made to ensure that the foundations rested on hard rock. The southern quay was resited further south which made the dock wider and enabled a mole to be constructed at the west end of the dock, equipped with its own low-level coal hoists and thus giving greater capacity. In addition to fixed hoists, moveable hoists were also installed to help with the positioning of vessels.

Thirty locomotives had been used in the construction of the dock and all the spoil excavated was re-used to form new structures involving continual laying of new tracks and their removal. At the peak, there were some 3,000 workers on site with work continuing by day and night during summer and autumn, much of the site being lit by electric light. The initial dock had a water area of 107 acres, this including the Basin and dry docks, the total cost of which was £2 million. Water was first let into the Dock on 29 June 1889 through the Basin on a rising tide, which covered the dock to a depth of five feet, the next tide covering eighteen feet and a third tide to twenty-three feet. The ceremonial opening of the Dock took place on 18 July 1889, with David Davies and the Earl of Plymouth and 2,000 invited guests, including all the leaders of the South Wales coal industry. The first vessel into the new dock was the SS Arno and six tips were ready for use. The same day all were in function with six vessels loaded ready for departure.

As with most dock facilities provided in South Wales at this time, the new Barry Dock was a victim of its own success with all the coal hoists operational. By 1893, a second dock had been authorised east of the original. Work began on this in 1894 and was completed ready for opening in 1898. The original dock became known as No. 1 or the Old Dock and the other as No. 2 or the New Dock, both names surviving into posterity. New Dock Offices were built between 1897 and 1900 by the architect Arthur E. Bell at a cost of

The west end of the Dock in 1889 with sailing and steam-driven vessels.

£59,000 to a design much replicated by other such buildings across the country.

During the five months of 1889 after the Dock opened, it handled 598 ships which took away 1.07 million tons of coal. This rose gradually each year until, by 1897, 2806 ships were handled and 5.85 million tons of coal exported. Barry vied with Cardiff Docks in terms of export coal tonnage and in the record year of 1913 actually overtook Cardiff, exporting over 11 million tons of coal, coke and patent fuel, including that for ships' bunkers. Following the First World War, the mid 1920s saw the start of the gradual reduction in the market for South Wales coal as vessels were converted to oil firing and continental countries began to

The C.H. Bailey Dry Dock with the Blue Star Liner Imperial Star undergoing repair in the rear section.

THE BLUE STAR LINER "IMPERIAL STAR" (572'3"x70'3" — g.r.t. 13,181) IN BAILEY DRYDOCK, BARRY.

The dock entrance with the lighthouse on the right.

Ships loading coal in the 1930s.

develop their own coal industries. Though export levels were still significant, they never again achieved their previous levels as South Wales coal, coke and patent fuel export (and coastwise) tonnages show: 1923, 101.6 million; 1929, 79.6 million; 1938, 48.3 million; 1960, 7.1 million.

Faced with such huge reductions in their coal business, the British Transport Docks Board needed to reduce the cost of dealing with their export and coastwise coal shipment for which they were carrying large amounts of spare capacity and in 1963 implemented a plan to concentrate all bituminous coal, coke and patent fuel at Barry Docks, with all anthracite at Swansea (which was the case anyway). This produced a hardly noticeable effect at Barry, such was the extent of the market decline and by the end of the decade, the traffic was virtually ended. An attempt to revive the business in the early 1970s with the construction of a coke conveyor to satisfy shipment markets from Nantgarw and Cwm Coke Ovens was short lived and soon both No. 1 and No. 2 Docks became reliant on other traffic for their future.

In the days of boom, Barry had handled significant amounts of general cargoes: timber, both for construction and pitprops for the mines, meat, flour, oil etc. and

had well reputed Dry Docks run by C.H. Bailey, where even smaller passenger liners could be accommodated and also Graving Docks; and from the late 1950s developed a significant new trade in Geest bananas whose vessels from the West Indies docked on Sunday afternoons; and until the following Wednesday a prolific activity in unloading bananas to rail vans ensued, their train departures starting sometimes on the Sunday night and continuing at normally three trains a day from Cadoxton Low Level Yard. However, in the late 1960s, Geest decided to leave Barry and move to Southampton, leaving a very big hole in the general cargo position at Barry.

The mid 1950s had seen the removal of the coal hoists from the east end of No. 2 Dock and their replacement by high capacity cranes and these were put to very good use during the 1960s handling bulk cargoes such as phosphate rock, iron and manganese ore and imported coal, all for long distance rail transport. But Barry's Achilles heel was the size of vessels it could accommodate through the Lady Windsor Lock or the Basin which was slightly larger, and with the increase in the size of the ships in the merchant fleet, the larger vessels used the larger docks at

An aerial view of No. 1 Dock in 1947. The Mole can be seen affording additional berths at the west end with oil storage tanks behind and the fresh water pond at the extreme right. Some tips had already been removed by now, such as the two on the cross-berth where two vessels are berthed on the top left. The Basin is top centre and the Junction-Cut to the New (No. 2) Dock top left. The curved tracks to the tips are in the centre, but generally business was poor when this post-war view was taken.
Author's Collection

An aerial view of No. 2 Dock in 1947. Barry Dock Station is on the bend far right centre west of the Storage Sidings from where the tips were fed with wagons to be unloaded into waiting vessels. Author's Collection.

A closer view of the west end of No. 1 Dock with ships loading at many berths and several laid up in the centre. The extent of coal traffic handled can be seen from the number of wagons in the foreground and on the tip roads, the view being between Barry and Barry Dock stations. Ships awaiting entry to the dock can be seen at the top in Barry Roads. Author's Collection.

An aerial view of No. 2 Dock showing the high capacity cranes which replaced the three coal tips at the east end of the dock in the 1950s. These were used to discharge phosphate rock, imported coal, iron and manganese ore during the 1960s. Rank's Flour Mill is in the centre with a banana boat from the West Indies in the top right. The buildings behind were former warehouses which had ceased to be used for that purpose and were now used by small concerns for various purposes. By now the tip roads serving many of the coal hoists on the No. 2 Dock had been recovered and the hoists dismantled, dating the picture to the late 1960s or early '70s.

Rank's Flour Mill on the south side of No. 2 Dock with a vessel unloading grain. In the mid-1950s, two sailing vessels the *Pamir* and the *Passat* operated this service.

A view from the Dock Offices in the 1990s looking down on the David Davies statue and the entrance to the disused Graving Dock and across to the Basin and the Dock Entrance.

The Fulham 1X entering the Dock in the early 1950s. The Fulham boats conveyed coastwise coal to power stations and were regular visitors to the Docks.

Loading Bargoed coal on a hoist at the west end of No. 1 Dock.

No. 1 Dock stands empty in the early 1990s. All the coal hoists have been removed but the berths are still intact, though soon to be removed. The land beyond would now be used for the Waterfront Development of houses and retail, this representing one hundred years in the history of Barry.

A Barry Railway F Class No. 135 heads for Graving Dock Junction on the Caisson lines passing the tip roads to No. 21 Tip in the 1920s. The Caisson lines ran across the swing bridge across the entrance to No. 2 Dock and then served the Timber Yards and the south side of No. 2 Dock. The engine may have come from the sidings serving the coal hoists on the Cross Berth which were removed in 1938.

Barry's 8481 passes the cranes at the east end of No. 2 Dock with the B36 afternoon freight to Cardiff Newtown in the early 1960s.

Barry Railway B1 Class 271 collecting empty wagons on the lines behind Rank's Mill in 1950.

Running from No. 2 Dock to Cardiff Pengam with a mixed freight, Barry's 6658 on turn J32 (formerly B32) round the bend at the west end of No. 2 Dock which will take it through Graving Dock Junction and on to Cadoxton Low Level, in this 1962 picture. Alastair Warrington.

6774 has dropped down into the Docks from Cadoxton Low Level, has just passed Graving Dock Junction and is now heading for the Caisson across the Junction Cut at the west end of No. 2 Dock, en route to serve the installations beyond.

Graving Dock Junction SB at the junction between the tracks from Nos 1 and 2 Docks. July 1966.

Barry's 8450 has just climbed from the No. 2 Dock lines to Cadoxton Low Level with a Barry Dock to Cardiff Newtown evening goods and now waits the road to proceed.

At the west end of No. 1, Dock Barry's 8497 brings a mixed goods from Cardiff Pengam into the terminating sidings, the wagons being for Barry Goods and various destinations on the Docks on 14 February 1953.

The low-level lines from Barry West into the west end of No. 1 Dock were used for turning 2-6-0 and LNW 0-8-0 tender engines off excursion traffic, the engines reversing up the incline from the dock lines past Barry Engine Works to the High Level. Here, 49121 off the Sunday Nantybwch excursion and now facing east approaches the reversing point.

Barry Goods was at the far west end of No. 1 Dock and in this 1964 view was being converted into a small conventionally run Coal Concentration Depot, absorbing the traffic from Barry Dock Syndicate Sidings, Cadoxton and Rhoose. The wide expanse of yard is being prepared to house wharfage facilities for the storage of domestic coal by coal merchants for whom coal wagons are in the yard. Also in the yard, wagons of wheels off rolling stock scrapped by Woodhams await despatch to a steel works, a traffic that will dominate forwarded traffic from Barry for several years, following the cessation of banana traffic.

Swansea, Cardiff, Newport and Bristol, especially where onward movement of the imported traffic required better access to the M4 motorway or shorter rail transport (e.g. for imported coal to Didcot Power Station which has since found its optimum home at Avonmouth).

Little by little, one market after another disappeared from Barry Docks until there was no case for the retention of No. 1 Dock. Flour traffic into Rank's Atlantic Flour Mill on No. 2 faced declining levels of business over many years and, though rebuilt with new state of the art equipment, closed in 2013 and was demolished in 2014. The only significant trade left at No. 2 Docks is of chemicals for Dow Corning at the east end of No. 2, their processed bitumen still being conveyed by daily trains to the north of England. Other traffic through No. 2 Dock,

the only operative section, is now a rarity, the dockside accommodation populated by small industrial concerns. No. 1 Dock area has now been converted into a successful residential and retail Waterfront development, with other enhancements, such as a Premier Inn and an extension of road facility to Barry Island, with the Dock still providing a few summer attractions in the form of visiting tall ships etc.

But overall, Barry has really felt the effect of the big wheel of history as it turned and left Barry Docks to find another future. One wonders what long term future the redundant No. 1 Dock and the struggling No. 2 Dock have, if any. Sea transport these days is all about deep water berths such as Milford Haven and ports capable of handling the huge container ships or the luxury cruise ships; and Barry does not tick any of those boxes.

Whaling vessels *Polar Maid* and *Ross Sea* discharging whale oil at the Cory Bros. installation on the Mole at the west end of No. 1 Dock.

CHAPTER 3

PORTS TO PORTS EXPRESS

THE DEVELOPMENT OF Barry Docks produced much passenger as well as coal traffic for the Company. An important element in this was the need to convey seamen arriving on ships into Barry to their home towns across the country and the reverse when seamen had to travel to Barry to join their ships. To provide for this traffic, the Barry Railway put forward a case to the GWR, Great Central and North Eastern Railways to provide a cross-country train from Barry to Newcastle and Hull, running via the Great Central line from Banbury and serving such important cities as Leicester, Nottingham and Sheffield, as it went. This train was introduced in 1905 and was soon extended to run through to and from Swansea. Power in the early years of the train would have been provided by the GWR 4-4-0 fleet, probably a Bulldog or Atbara, but by the 1930s this had changed to the 4300 Class 2-6-0 as the route had been changed to run via Cheltenham requiring a smaller engine which worked through between Banbury (where the Great Central engine was changed) and Swansea. This was a long run for a secondary main line engine and was one of the reasons for the development of the Manor Class 4-6-0 by Swindon. The first engines of the class were allocated to Banbury for this working. Stock for the train was provided on alternate days by the GWR and LNER, including a restaurant car. In the 1920s, the train ran via Penarth, the down train the 9.30am

Newcastle to Swansea leaving Cardiff Gen. at 6.50pm after an eleven minute station stop, and calling at Penarth at 7.00 to 7.02, Barry Docks 7.15 to 7.16pm and Barry 7.19 to 7.21pm. The up train left Swansea at 7.30am and called at Barry at 8.54 to 8.56am, Barry Docks at 9.00 to 9.02am and Penarth at 9.17 to 9.20am before being at Cardiff Gen. from 9.30 to 9.35am.

The train ceased to run via Barry in 1939, running main line from Swansea to Cardiff, and was also cut back in terms of days run. By the 1950s, it ran on Fridays and Saturdays only, terminating at York on Saturdays, worked as far Banbury by a Landore Castle which gave way there to an ER V2 2-6-0 which worked on to Sheffield. By now the sea-faring nature of the service had been lost and it was provided merely within the cross-country framework. With the Beeching closure of the Great Central route, the routing was removed, but there was also a service from Cardiff to Newcastle at 8.30am via the former LMS route through Birmingham.

At the time, this was the only main line express running through Barry. After its withdrawal, during the 1940s and early '50s, there was a SO service from Barry Island to Birmingham at approximately 9.30am, worked by a Saint Class 4-6-0, but this ceased by about 1952, following which the only main line expresses to be seen at Barry were on excursions and diversions.

Banbury Mogul 6369 leaves Porthkerry Tunnel with the up Ports to Ports express with the Great Central stock train in 1936. J.G.Hubback/John Hodge Collection.

Great Central stock is again on this down service, complete with roofboards, as it leaves Porthkerry Tunnel and rounds a bend in Porthkerry Park in 1936. J.G. Hubback/John Hodge Collection.

The down Ports to Ports Express with GWR stock in 1939 passing Barry Sidings in the charge of Banbury Manor 7811 Dunley Manor, based at Banbury until March 1946. J.G. Hubback/John Hodge Collection.

The down train leaving Porthkerry Tunnel on the canted track behind 7811 Dunley Manor in 1939, with Great Central coaching stock. J.G. Hubback/John Hodge Collection.

The up train has just crossed Porthkerry Viaduct in 1939 behind a Banbury Manor, and will soon make its next call at Barry. J.G. Hubback/John Hodge Collection.

In the 1930s and after the War there was a 9.30am Summer Saturdays only through train from Barry Island to Birmingham to take returning holiday makers to save them transferring at Cardiff General. In the latter 1930s the train is seen between Barry and Barry Docks hauled by Canton's 2983 *Redgauntlet*.

CHAPTER 4

MOTIVE POWER TRANSITION AT BARRY 1920-1930

THE BARRY RAILWAY was probably the most vulnerable with regard to the effect of the Grouping, the amalgamation with the GWR, in terms of motive power. The Barry had a variety of wheel arrangements and non-standard features which would have been anathema to the highly standardised GWR at the time, while their fleet had been very hard pressed both before and during the war years by the intensive duties that engines and men were expected to perform. The verdict of the GWR Boiler Inspector when he visited Barry at the Grouping is proof of that situation. It was not perhaps surprising that Swindon took a heavy toll on the Barry fleet of engines once they got to grips with the task of sorting out the vast number of tank engines taken over from the private companies.

In November 1922, fifteen GW pannier and saddle tanks were sent to Barry, including seven ex-Swindon and two ex-Wolverhampton, doubtless to cover a shortage of power due to the number of Barry engines under works overhaul. Some may well have been for repair themselves in Barry Works, as eight had gone in January and February 1923 and details in the GWR Allocation Ledgers of the time do not make the position clear. Four were of the 1501 Class which were used for passenger work and these were the longest to remain, 1521 going to Cathays in April 1923, 1535 to Newport in August and 1544 to Treherbert in June, with 1557 having gone to Cathays in February, possibly after works repair. The longest to stay were an 1854 Class (1714) until May 1923, a 1661 Class (1661 itself)

and an 1854 Class (1760) both remaining at Barry until December 1923. Other than these, all those arriving in November 1922 had gone by March 1923.

For the first three years after the Grouping in 1922, there was little effect in terms of withdrawal on the Barry's stock of passenger and coal engines. During 1923, only one of their F Class was withdrawn (possibly quite unrelated to the later situation). The fleet remained intact during 1924 and suffered only two losses (a Class G 0-4-4T and an H 0-8-2T) in 1925. The axe was however to fall heavily in 1926 with seventeen withdrawals, though it must be said that ten of these were the entire Class L 0-6-4Ts which had a propensity to derail on points. Some have said this was an unnecessarily harsh decision to withdraw what were almost new engines, which could have been rebuilt to a GWR standard design; but with a need for a macro approach on the subject of future design for the Valleys (the 5600 Class), Swindon may well have decided to sacrifice the ten Ls to the more important cause.

Six more Barrys were withdrawn in 1927, nine during 1928, one in 1929 and nine in 1930, leaving only the B and B1 and F classes intact, with just a few odd examples of other classes, all of which would in fact disappear by the end of 1932. It was somewhat ironic that the last of the Barry 'oddities' to go in May 1932 was one of the first A Class 0-6-0Ts built when the line was opened in 1888. The two C Class 2-4-2Ts (renumbered 1322/3) had been moved to Aberdare and Cathays respectively and were withdrawn in May 1928 and August 1926. The four D Class 0-8-0s (renumbered 1387-90) were withdrawn between late 1927 and mid-1930. The F Class 0-6-0T shunters had found favour at Cathays, Pill, Cardiff East Dock and Duffryn Yard and only a couple remained at Barry. I have the strong feeling that the GWR were using these to develop the future 67XX shunter widely used on the South Wales Docks.

The four G Class 0-4-4T passenger engines were all gone by mid-1929, and the intriguing powerful H Class 0-8-2Ts by the end of 1930. The eleven J Class passenger 2-4-2Ts went progressively between 1926 and 1930, the Ls all together in 1926 and the five attractive K Class 0-6-2Ts between 1927-32.

In January 1920, two of the GWR 3100 Class 2-6-2Ts were loaned or hired by the GWR to the Barry Railway Company, presumably to help out with the heavy coal service requirement faced by that company, probably in the face of many of its own heavy-duty engines being out of

service following the war years. The 3100 Class had been introduced from January 1905 (following extensive trials with the prototype No.99) for heavy coal duties and passenger working in the Newport Valleys, for passenger services and banking elsewhere in GW territory, and for banking through the Severn Tunnel and up Sapperton.

On 11 January 1920, No.3119 is recorded as transferred from Newport Ebbw Junction to the Barry Company, with No. 3140 similarly transferred from Canton on the 17th. Both engines received some unknown attention at Canton between 10 and 28 August 1920 before returning to Barry. No.3140 was transferred back to Canton in October 1920 and was joined by No.3119 in March 1921 in exchange for No.3129 which left Canton for Barry in March. No.3177 had also been transferred from Canton to Barry in February 1921 and was returned in September. Thus, by the end of September 1921, their presence at Barry had terminated – temporarily.

In 1920-24, Barry received first two, then six of the 3100 Class. Here 3131 stands in the yard at the back of the shed in 1924, but all were transferred away, back to Ebbw Jn. in October 1924. Note the L Class on the extreme left. Author's Collection.

On 10 April 1922, three 31s were again transferred to Barry, Nos. 3129 from Canton, 3163 from Old Oak Common and 3164 from Canton. During their stay at Barry, each of these three received a heavy overhaul at Swindon (from November 1922 to March 1923, April to August 1923, and October 1923 to January 1924 respectively), each returning to Barry. They were joined by four others of the class, No.3131 from Ebbw Junction in November 1923, 3132 ex-Swindon Works in December 1923, 3150 from Severn Tunnel the same month, and 3181 ex-Swindon Works in February 1924. No.3150 left to go for heavy repair at Swindon in September 1924, leaving the other six in residence. The history of the class at Barry came to an abrupt end in October 1924 when all six were transferred to Ebbw Junction on the 8th, 10th and 11th. They were probably allocated for passenger and coal services and would have proved very useful for Sunday excursion traffic to Barry Island.

In April 1922, four of the 4200 Class 2-8-0T freight engines were allocated to Barry and these were joined in October 1922 by four new engines direct from Swindon Works Nos. 4296-99. Two others arrived in January 1923 with another in October. When the 3100 Class engines were all transferred away in October 1924, they were replaced by no fewer than eleven new 52XXs which had spent only a short time at Newport. The arrival of the eleven 52XXs brought the total number of 2-8-0Ts at Barry to a resounding twenty-four by the end of 1924, of which three or four were outbased at Trehafod. At this time, the 42s were the GWR's Valleys freight engine, but in later years became more associated with the Newport Valleys where they dominated the coal traffic. However, during the 1920s and early '30s they worked from Barry (and also Cathays) into the Cardiff Valleys in significant numbers, with sixteen still on the books at Barry in 1932, but the numbers reducing as new 66XXs entered

service, such that by Nationalisation only one solitary 42XX remained at Barry.

When the 5600 Class entered service in 1925, Barry received a substantial allocation at the outset, including No.5600 itself, fresh from its ignominious entry on the scene at Swindon Works when an embarrassing valve design failure had to be urgently rectified. Fifteen were allocated to Barry by the start of 1926 and 1927, rising to twenty-five (and often a few more) from 1928 until 1935. Though the 42s had virtually disappeared from Barry by Nationalisation, there were now twenty-six 56s allocated.

The Taff Vale Class As really took over the passenger working at Barry from the end of 1928 when the former Taff Vale shed at Penarth Dock closed and most of the As on its books were moved at Barry. However, the GWR had tried out the As much earlier at Barry and in December 1923 two were sent on trial until March 1924 (Nos.388 and 401, which would actually become two long-standing Barry engines, No.401 becoming 303 in later renumbering). Three more As spent periods at Barry during 1924 (345 – another future long-term Barry engine – from June to November, 346 from March to July and 382 - which had a glowing reputation there in future years – from May to December.

There was however no presence of TV As at Barry during the whole of 1925, actually until September 1926, though several passed through Barry Works and would have been run in from the shed. Three spent short periods at Barry between September 1926 and year end, but 344 remained there from September 1926 until October 1927. Seven more were allocated for various periods during 1927, but from September/October 1928 the closure of Penarth Dock saw what became the Barry allocation of As for many years take root there, with fifteen allocated until the 1950s. It is however amazing how many long-term residents of both the As and 56s there were at Barry, a feature, it

In the late 1920s, four or five of the 3900 Class 2-6-2T were based at Barry. Here, 3908 stands in the yard, probably in 1928/9. Author's Collection.

A group of four TV Class as at the back of the shed, 357, 375, 372 and 382 all coaled ready on Sunday 24 January 1954 for their work on Monday morning. John Hodge.

A rare photograph of one of the 3901 Class allocated to Barry, passing Palmerston with the Barry to Llandrindod Wells service via Merthyr in the mid-1930s.

must be said, shared with other Valleys sheds.

The late 1920s had seen the transfer of several of the 39XX 2-6-2Ts from the Birmingham area to South Wales, where they worked the Rhondda & Swansea Bay services between Treherbert and Swansea for a few years. In October 1927, Nos.3905/15 were transferred from Danygraig to Barry for trials on the Barry-Cardiff service. These were joined by Nos. 3908/9/13 in early 1928. No.3915 left for Swindon Works in November 1929 and did not return but the other four all remained at Barry until withdrawn, three towards the end of 1930 and the final one (No.3913) in June 1931. Unfortunately, very few photographs exist of the working of this class at Barry, there being only one resident railway photographer there at the time – J.G. Hubback – who

unfortunately preferred to photograph main line engines rather than the locals.

Though never based at Barry, another Great Western class allocated to the area was the 3600 2-4-2T. There had been odd examples of this class at Newport, Cardiff and Bridgend/Tondu for several years, but the late 1920s and early '30s saw several based at Canton and often employed on those Barry and Vale of Glamorgan services worked by Canton, using H targets, before Canton surrendered all its passenger work on the Barry and Penarth lines to Cathays. It was perhaps surprising that none were ever allocated to Barry in view of the Barry Company's association with the 2-4-2T wheel design. All those based at Canton were withdrawn during 1930-32, no doubt overtaken by the superior new 5600 Class.

CHAPTER 5

LATER RAILWAY DEVELOPMENTS

IN 1927, THE GWR prepared plans of the whole of the Barry layout, divided into four sections, the first showing the area around Barry station, shed and works, the second between the Works and Barry Dock station including coal tips, the third showing Barry Dock Storage Sidings and coal tips, and the fourth the east end of the Storage Sidings and Cadoxton. These are now shown.

A 1927 plan of the west end of the Barry layout showing Barry Junction with the Vale of Glamorgan and Barry Island branch, Barry Station, Engine Shed and Carriage Shed (top left), West Pond (later filled in and used by Woodham for storage of condemned engines in the 1960s), Barry Engine Works, Carriage Works, Wagon Repair Shops, Goods Depot, North Hydraulic Station, and west end of No. 1 Dock (right), plus extensive storage sidings. Courtesy R.A. Cooke.

A 1927 plan of the section from Barry Engine Works to Barry Dock station showing the feed lines to each of the tips (Nos. 1-11) on No. 1 Dock with the High Level Storage Sidings. These were used from the 1930s for storing empty stock off excursions to Barry Island on Sundays and Bank Holidays. The sidings running alongside the dock were at road level with the tip mechanism above. The Graving Docks can be seen bottom right. Barry Dock SB just west of the station is far right.
Courtesy R.A. Cooke.

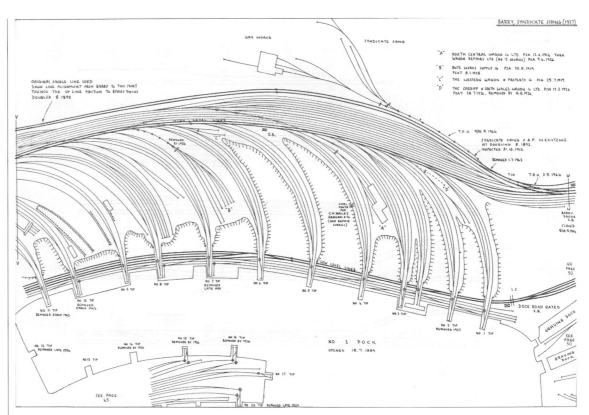

A 1927 plan from Barry Dock Station to No. 29 Tip on No. 2 Dock. Showing the Graving Docks and Low Level Lines running into tunnels (through Graving Dock Jn.) under Barry Dock Storage Sidings between Barry Dock Station and Cadoxton. This was the view from our house in Dock View Road.
Courtesy R.A. Cooke.

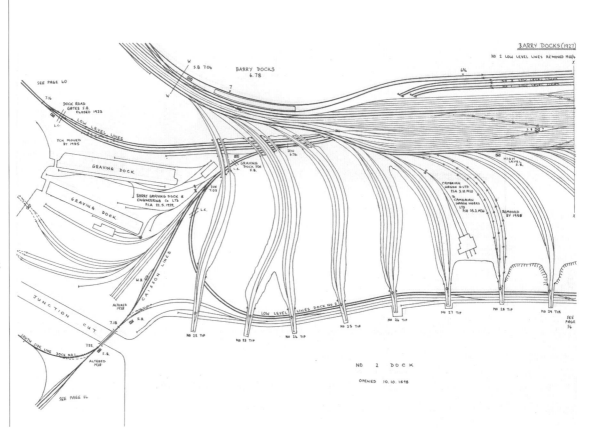

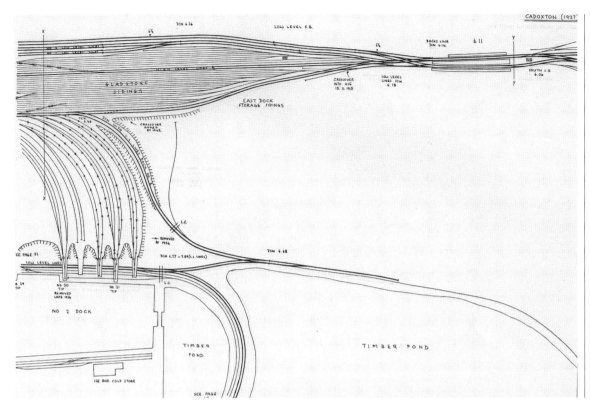

CADOXTON (1927)

A 1927 plan of the east end of the Barry Dock complex showing the Storage Sidings (Gladstone Sidings) approaching Cadoxton station, Tips Nos. 30 and 31 at the east end of No. 2 (replaced by high capacity cranes), and the Timber Pond. Courtesy R.A. Cooke.

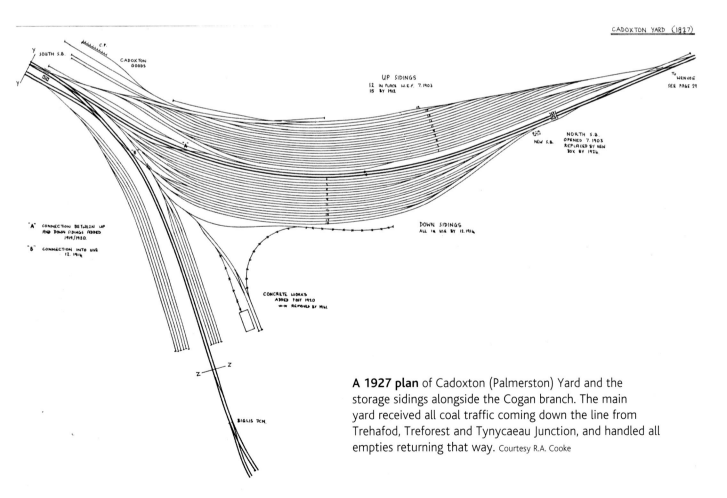

CADOXTON YARD (1927)

A 1927 plan of Cadoxton (Palmerston) Yard and the storage sidings alongside the Cogan branch. The main yard received all coal traffic coming down the line from Trehafod, Treforest and Tynycaeau Junction, and handled all empties returning that way. Courtesy R.A. Cooke

Because of the huge expenditure on the 1914-18 war effort, maintenance and repair of the railways had been cut back and the independent private companies were in a bad state at the cessation of hostilities. In 1922, the smaller railway companies were amalgamated into the four major ones and the Barry Company became part of the Great Western Railway in April 1922. This opened up many cases for the closure of duplicate routes, especially in the Valleys where such duplication was rife and in 1930, the newly created routes across the Llanbradach (Duffryn Isaf) and Penyrheol Viaducts were closed and the viaducts dismantled.

Excursion traffic to Barry Island expanded considerably during the 1920s and for the Summer season 1929 a new island platform was opened at Barry Island, for which a new signal box at Barry Island East was necessary. But there were also cutbacks and in July 1930, the former Barry Railway stations at Treforest and Pontypridd Graig were closed to passenger traffic, the former Taff Vale stations at both places replacing them. The passenger facilities along that line at Wenvoe, Creigiau and Efail Isaf were also cut back with only a couple of trains per day retained, the line being completely closed in 1962, when the huge coal shipment holding sidings at Palmerston (Cadoxton) were also closed and recovered. Though bituminous coal shipment for South East Wales was concentrated at Barry Docks from 1963, this was easily handled at Barry Dock Storage Sidings between Barry Dock and Cadoxton stations, such had been the reduction in the volume of export and coastwise shipment traffic and by the end of the decade shipment coal traffic through Barry had virtually ceased.

Following the demise of the last Barry Railway F Class in 1937, superseded by the docks shunter GWR 6700 Class from 1930, the only former Barry Railway engines left in traffic were a few of the B and many of the B1 side tank 0-6-2Ts, most of which were by now relegated to light freight and shunting work, with the heavier coal working having passed to the more powerful 5600 Class. The last of the B Class went in October 1949, and 1951 was to see the last of the B1 Class, the final four going in April 1951.

From 1928, when Penarth Dock depot was closed, until Nationalisation, passenger working on the Barry to Cardiff, Vale of Glamorgan and Pontypridd lines was largely in the hands of the former Taff Vale Class As, assisted by the 5600 Class. The 2-6-2 tanks, a scarce possession on the GWR, re-visited Barry by Nationalisation, when No.5195 was allocated from the Birmingham area followed by 5183. In September 1948 three new 41s were allocated (the now preserved 4160 with 4161/3, later joined by 4177), so Barry then enjoyed a period of six Prairie tanks, until the autumn of 1953.

In September 1953, the Cardiff Valleys passenger service was completely reorganised and a highly successful regular interval service instituted. A fleet of Standard Class 3 2-6-2Ts, transferred from the Birmingham area (Nos. 82000-09) was first based at Barry, with services from Treherbert and on the Rhymney Valley worked by 5101 Class and 5600 Class, with the Rhymneys ably assisted by the AP Class 0-6-2Ts (No. 78-83). The Barry allocation of Prairie tanks was transferred to Rhymney, except for one, the much prized 4177, which was kept for the 3.30pm to Treherbert (BC). Soon some Standard Class 3s were allocated to Treherbert and the fleet was renewed by Swindon built Nos. 82032-44 with enlarged coal bunkers, as there had been problems with some turns having to return to shed for re-coaling. The original fleet of 82000-09 were all transferred away, mainly to the Bristol area, the last to go being 82003 which was employed on Barry turn BE for an extended period. Though use of the Barry TV Class As on

First of the class 82000, then based at Treherbert, with the 11.35am Sunday Barry to Treherbert on 30 October 1955.

82002 awaits departure from Barry with a morning service to Llantwit Major in 1954, with the BD target.

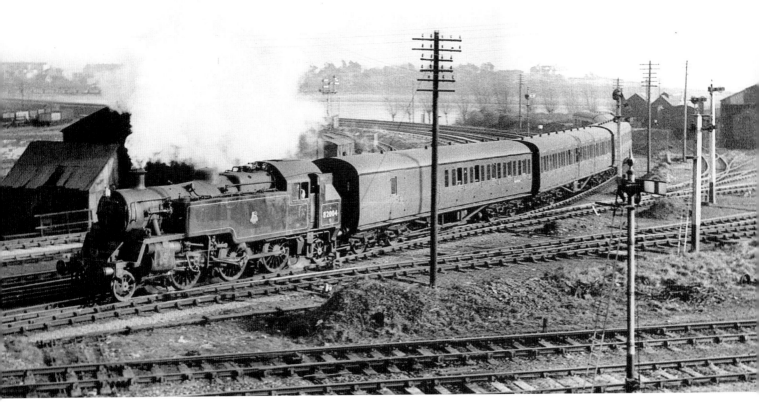

Shortly after the start of the Regular Interval service, 82004 rounds the bend into Barry station with the 4.5pm Barry Island to Queen Street in October 1953.

The 4.30pm Treherbert to Barry Island runs into Barry behind 82033 on target TC, forming the 6.30pm return.

passenger work ceased as from September 1953, use of Cathays As continued with four turns on the Barry line until the As were withdrawn from service gradually from 1956. Though the Standard Class 3s were popular with crews, they were underpowered and whenever a seven-coach load was required to work up the Rhondda as on some Saturdays, the Cathays turn CB (which was later covered from Radyr by an 82), had to be worked by a 56XX (see also fuller details under Passenger Services section). I always thought it a pity that the WR never tried the Standard Class 4 (80XXX) 2-6-4T on the Cardiff Valleys as their extra power would have proved very useful and they were very successful elsewhere. I have a strong feeling that some motive power people remembered the Barry Railway Class L 0-6-4T and their propensity to derail on points (see also fuller details under Passenger Services section).

The year 1958 saw the introduction of three Car DMU services on some of the Barry turns, as a straight swap for the steam diagrams, an earlier DMU design having been already introduced on the Eastern and Western Valleys.

Gradually, the whole of the main passenger services on the Rhondda, Rhymney and Barry lines became covered by DMUs and the steam fleets, still mostly made up of relatively new or still able engines, was transferred away. The Dowlais line services, Vale of Neath and Brecon & Merthyr remained steam dominated until closure.

The year 1959 saw the closure of Barry Engine Works, as the number of steam engines on the Western Region began to decline with the dieselisation of the local services, shunting and main line in the West of England. The closure of the MT&A line from Merthyr to Abergavenny and the withdrawal of passenger services on the Sirhowy Valley from June 1960

Barry's 82036 pulls away from Barry station with the 5.30pm Treherbert to Barry Island, forming the 7.30pm return. The Carriage Shed can be seen on the right.

New DMUs of Class 118 entered service on the Cardiff Valleys in 1958 and here a brand new set enters Cadoxton station on a train from Barry Island to Queen Street on 25 May 1958, with the coal hoists of No. 2 Dock clearly visible in the background.

A view from Barry signal box of a DMU running into the bay platform ready to form an outgoing service on 25 September 1960.

brought about an end to excursion traffic from there to Barry Island, and this was followed only two years later by the end of passenger services on the Eastern and Western Valleys in April 1962, which significantly reduced the number of excursions to Barry Island on weekends and bank holidays, this now being reduced to trains from the Rhondda and Rhymney Valleys. This was then further reduced by the closure of the Vale of Neath as a through route in 1964 and by the following Beeching cuts affecting the Maerdy, Senghenydd and Aberdare branches, so that all that was left of the traffic to Barry Island was contained within the Cardiff Valleys DMU service, plus main line and services from Newport. This erosion of the day-tripper traffic was accompanied by the larger exodus of the holiday market to air travel to Continental Europe, and Barry Island was in terminal decline.

Steam power came to end in South Wales in 1965 but most depots closed during 1964, though at Barry this was difficult to tell as many condemned and stored engines arrived at this time, those stored being held at the shed. By this time, there were many condemned engines held on the West Pond site and around Barry Works, where the sidings were rented to Woodhams for storage of condemned engines.

In 1969, it was announced that the line between Barry Town and Barry Island was to be singled, marking the absolute death knell of what had previously totalled some 30,000 day trippers a day and a service in and out every 5 minutes.

A new generation of DMUs was introduced in the 1980s to replace those introduced into the area in 1958. The previous three-car sets with a seating capacity of 262, were replaced by two-car sets with 147 seats in the Sprinter Class 150 units and up to 121 seats in the bus-type Pacers and these survive to this day. Overcrowding is now rife when only two cars are provided on peak hour services where previously six cars with seating for 524 were provided. Peak hour services on the Barry line, of which I still have experience, is uncomfortable and unhealthy with the number of passengers crammed into the carriages. On the 8.06am from Rhoose, no one joining at Barry and beyond can get a seat! These points will be expanded on in the next section on Passenger Services.

Llanbradach Viaduct which stretched from Penrhos on the Rhymney Railway to Duffryn Isaf on the Brecon & Merthyr, built by the Barry Rly. and demolished by the GWR in 1930's.

CHAPTER 6

PASSENGER SERVICES

THE BARRY RAILWAY took great pride in its passenger services with first the 0-4-4T G Class and then the 2-4-2T J Class as the nominated passenger engines, though the service was begun with the 0-6-0 A Class and ended with the 0-6-4T L Class playing a part. Passenger stock was owned by the Barry but was sometimes bought in from other railways and in the days of 4 and 6 wheelers, it was common to see trains of ten coaches. At the Grouping in 1922, there were thirty-five weekday trains from Barry to Cardiff General, including the 7.30am Ports to Ports Swansea to Newcastle express, which called at Barry at 8.54 to 8.56am and Barry Docks at 9.00 to 9.02am, then running non-stop to Cardiff via Penarth where it called at 9.17 to 9.20am, at that time hauled by a Bulldog 4-4-0. The routing via Penarth occurred for only a few years and the whole service ceased in 1939.

At the Grouping in 1922/23, there were twelve sets of coaches working the Barry Railway passenger service:-

Sets 1, 2 & 4 Each 10 coaches (4 & 6 wheelers) Barry-Cardiff/Llantwit Major.

Set 3 7 Bogie Coaches Barry-Cardiff/Llantwit Major.

Set 5 8 coaches Barry-Llantwit Major SO.

Set 6 7 coaches Barry-Cardiff.

Set B1 7 coaches Barry Cardiff/Bridgend/Porth.

Set CP1 5 coaches working Pontypridd-Clarence Road.

Set PO 7 coaches working Barry-Porth.

Set PW 7 coaches 3rd Class Only Workmen.

Vestibule Train Barry-Bridgend.

Motor Set Barry-Wenvoe/Llantwit Major.

The operation was covered by eleven engines from Barry, one from Hafod and one from Bridgend.

In Barry Rly. days No. 98 rounds the bend from the Barry Island branch into Barry station with a train to Cardiff.

Barry Railway B1 Class No. 60 makes a fine start from Barry station with a Vale train to either Llantwit Major or Bridgend. Engines ran either way round on services to Cardiff or Bridgend until September 1953 when they always ran engine first up the Valley to Merthyr and Treherbert.

A busy scene at Barry station in the early years of the century with a train standing in the bay platform, passengers awaiting a train at the up platform and trains at both down platforms."

No. 98 standing at the up platform at Barry with a train to Cardiff.

No. 86 runs into Cardiff Riverside platform with a train from Clarence Road to Pontypridd on 11 August 1913.

No. 97 at Cardiff Riverside with a train from Barry to Clarence Road on 11 August 1913.

No. 88 leaves Dinas Powis with a Cardiff to Barry Island train in the 1920s formed of ten ex-Lancashire & Yorkshire 4 wheelers.
J. Pitt/Author's Collection.

Barry Station Yard and platforms c1950 with a train set and various coaches in the yard. The two coaches on the far left are from Barry Coach Works and the van is standing at the loading dock where vans of cattle were received and any other traffic requiring road transfer was handled such as circus traffic for Romilly Park. The view shows the layout up to Barry Engine and Coach Works left centre with No. 1 Dock and the fresh water pond on the right. J.G. Hubback/John Hodge Collection.

The whole of the station yard was converted into a car park and is now a critical part of the facility offered at the station, often being almost completely full.

Barry Station looking east from the west end with the junction of the Island Branch and Vale of Glamorgan in the foreground.
B.W.L. Brooksbank.

Barry Station Signal Box, recently closed and demolished in 2015 with the opening of the Cardiff Signalling Centre.

Barry Station seen from the Ship Hill road bridge with a Class 143 Pacer unit departing for Barry Island and Class 37 diesels in the sidings for use on Aberthaw Power Station MGR trains. The former engine shed is in use as a maintenance and repair depot for MGR wagons.

Barry Dock down platform in the snow with the Dock Offices in the background.

The service changed little in number during the days of the GWR, with thirty-seven weekday trains in place of the Barry's thirty-five. The very early 4.50am was started at 5.10am and services recast in timing thereafter. Trains ran via Dinas Powis, with passengers changing at Cadoxton for an onward journey via Penarth. This service survived until Nationalisation in 1948, using the former Riverside Platforms 8 and 9 at Cardiff General, several services continuing to Clarence Road, leaving passengers for Queen Street and beyond to change to Platform 6 which had starting trains to the Valleys plus some through trains from Cadoxton/Penarth to the Valleys, a leave-over from the Taff Vale service. This rather untidy arrangement was well addressed by the introduction of the Cardiff Valleys Regular Interval Service by Leslie Morgan, the Divisional

Operating Manager, in September 1953. Under the new service, trains ran through from Treherbert and Merthyr to Barry Island, forming a regular interval service from Cardiff General Platform 7 to Barry Island at 11 and 41mins past each hour, returning from Barry Island on the hour and half past, the service on the hour to Merthyr and on the half hour to Treherbert. Some services from Rhymney also ran through to Barry or Barry Island, and normally returned to Rhymney via Penarth, while Clarence Road was served mainly by peak hour trains, some from and to Llantwit Major and Bridgend. Under this service, the number of weekday trains from Barry to Cardiff rose to forty-nine, with a few more in the reverse direction.

One of the principles of the services was to allocate work through to Barry Island to as many Valley depots as possible in

A wide angle view looking across from Old Mill Road of Cadoxton Mileage Yard, now used only for domestic coal traffic, with a 56XX taking the Cogan line with a return Sunday evening train from Barry Island. No. 2 Dock forms the background.

order to preserve their route knowledge, with Treherbert, Merthyr, Abercynon, Rhymney, Cathays (and later Radyr) all involved in the Interval Service, while Maerdy, Aberdare and Dowlais worked in on excursion traffic, as did Ebbw Junction, Aberbeeg and Severn Tunnel Junction Canton's involvement with the Barry line occurred largely on main line diversions, in which they were joined by Landore, and to lesser degree on freight working by Neath and Duffryn Yard and to a greater degree in later years with inter-works steel movements by Margam.

Details of the working of each of the up trains from Barry with the appropriate depot working for the train make interesting reading, over sixty years on from the introduction:

5.00am Barry-Cardiff Gen. Barry BE 82XXX

5.15am -Cardiff Gen. Barry BA 45XX Auto

5.35am -Treherbert Barry BB 82XXX

6.05am -Merthyr Barry BC 82XXX

6.46am -Queen St. Cathays 56XX (6.18am Llantwit Mjr.)

6.52am -Aberdare Barry BF 82XXX

7.15am Barry Is.-Clarence Rd. Barry BE 82XXX

7.30am -Treherbert Treherbert TB 51XX then 82XXX

8.00am -Clarence Rd. Barry BD 82XXX

8.29am Barry-Clarence Rd. Cathays CH TV A (8.03am ex-Llantwit Mjr.)

8.30am Barry Is.-Treherbert Treherbert TC 51XX then 82XXX

9.00am -Merthyr Cathays 56XX

9.30am -Treherbert Barry BB 82XXX

10.00am -Merthyr Barry BC 82XXX

10.30am -Treherbert Treherbert TA 51XX then 82XXX

10.44am Barry -Cardiff Gen. Treherbert TH TV A, then 56XX

11.00am Barry Is.-Merthyr Barry BF 82XXX

11.30am -Treherbert Treherbert TC 51XX then 82XXX

12noon -Merthyr Merthyr MA 82XXX (provided by Barry)

12.30pm -Treherbert Treherbert TC 51XX then 82XXX

1.00pm -Merthyr Abercynon JD TV A then 56XX

1.23pm Barry -Rhymney Rhymney RH 41XX

1.30pm Barry Is.-Treherbert Barry BD 82XXX

2.00pm -Merthyr Cathays TV A then 56XX

2.30pm -Treherbert Cathays CB 56XX

3.00pm -Merthyr Barry BB(2) 82XXX

3.30pm -Treherbert Barry BC(2) 4177

3.35pm -Rhymney Rhymney RA 41XX

3.45pm -Treherbert Treherbert TD 56XX

4.00pm -Clarence Rd. Barry BF 82XXX

4.05pm -Clarence Rd. Merthyr MC 82XXX (provided by Barry)

4.30pm -Treherbert Treherbert TA(2) 51XX then 82XXX

4.55pm Barry to Pontypridd Barry BG 45XX

5.00pm Barry Is.-Rhymney Rhymney RG 41XX

5.16pm Barry-Clarence Rd. Barry BE 82XXX (4.25pm Bridgend)

5.30pm Barry Is.-Treherbert Treherbert TB(2) 51XX then 82XXX

6.00pm -Merthyr Merthyr MA 82XXX (provided by Barry)

6.30pm -Treherbert Treherbert TC(2) 51XX then 82xxx

6.36pm -Queen St. Cathays CA TV A then 56xx

7.00pm -Merthyr Barry BB(2) 82XXX

7.30pm -Treherbert Barry BC (2) 4177

8.00pm -Merthyr Barry BF 82XXX (after recoaling)

8.30pm -Treherbert Treherbert TA(2) 51XX then 82XXX

9.05pm Barry- Merthyr Cathays CJ TV A then 56XX (Off 7.40 Bgd)

9.30pm Barry Is.-Treherbert Treherbert TB(2) 51XX then 82XXX

10.00pm -Merthyr Merthyr MA 82XXX (provided by Barry)

10.30pm -Treherbert Treherbert TC(2) 51XX then 82XXX

n Barry Island to Merthyr CE was a Cathays turn in steam days of the Regular Interval service and here their TV Class A 347 leaves
and with that train on 14 May 1955.

The 11am Merthyr to Barry Island JD, returning with the 1pm, was an Abercynon turn for which a TV Class A was used until their demise. Here their 386, a former Barry engine, passes Gladstone Bridge alongside the Western Welsh garage, with the down train.

An excellent vantage point to photograph trains with their engines working quite hard was through the railings near Ship Hill bridge with trains having to pull hard round the curve from the Barry Island branch. Here, Cathays 307 is steaming well as it hauls the 6.36pm Barry Island to Queen Street.

Another view from same spot as Cathays recently ex-works 305 is working the same train.

Ground level shots first of 305 and then 346 at the same spot, rounding the bend from Barry Island with the 6.36pm Barry Island to Queen Street.

Running into Barry Docks station with the Graving Dock in the background, 305 on the 6.36pm Barry Island to Queen Street.

Treherbert's 4177 with the 10.44am Barry to Cardiff Gen. passing the Western Welsh Garage on 18 June 1958.

Treherbert's 5162 with the 6.30pm Barry Island to Treherbert rounding the bend from the Barry Island branch on 7 August 1955.

The 10.35am Sunday Barry to Queen Street was auto worked by a Cathays engine. Here, the 5534 leaves the bay platform at Barry with the train on 4 May 1958.

The 9.30am Sunday Treherbert to Barry returned as here with the 11.35am Barry to Treherbert and was formed with the Rhondda & Swansea Bay stock which made the train at Treherbert, the only known case of such working. Here Treherbert's 5688 leaves Barry with the northbound train on 12 May 1957.

Following the demise of the Taff Vale Class As from passenger working, they were replaced by 56XXs as here with Cathays 6647 leaving Barry with the 5.23pm Cardiff Gen. to Barry Island, a previous stronghold of the As on 6 August 1957.

The 11am Barry
Island to Merthyr
leaves Barry Dock
behind Barry's 5664
on turn BF on 10
June 1957.

The Aberdare engine off Aberdare excursion No. 19 on Summer Sundays worked passenger services between Barry Island and Queen St. before going to shed for servicing pending return to Aberdare. Here, 6605 leaves Cadoxton on the down journey from Queen Street on 25 May 1958.

The 1.30pm Sunday Barry Island to Queen Street runs into Cadoxton behind Cathays 5687 on turn CA in 1958.

With shipment coal traffic still in evidence on the many sidings at Cadoxton, 82043 leaves with the 10am Barry Island to Merthyr, target BC, in 1956, its second trip of the day to Merthyr. Barry always took a pride in the appearance of their passenger engines as seen here.

82037 leaves Barry
Dock station with the 12noon Barry Island to Merthyr, target MA, on 7 August 1957. Barry provided two 82XXXs to Merthyr each day to work their MA and MC diagrams.

The Regular Interval Service remained untouched (at Leslie Morgan's instruction) until four years after the introduction of diesel multiple units in 1958. By this time, I had joined the Cardiff District Train Office in 1961 and was working on the Valley service some of the time. In 1963, I made the case to Jack Brennan, the Operating Officer, that we should devote attention to tidying up the working, providing six cars where only three were currently, and vice versa, particularly on the Rhymney service. There were still forty-six services provided between Barry and Cardiff, and soon we were to feel the effects of the Beeching cuts with the Vale of Glamorgan, Porth-Maerdy, Aberdare-Abercynon and the Vale of Neath service affected. There was widespread criticism of these cuts among staff at the DMO, as the Vale of Glamorgan line had to be kept open as the main line diversionary route between Cardiff and Bridgend, and the Aberdare branch was an important part of the valley network; but the London decision held sway. How interesting that history has now proved them wrong in the long term and both services, as well as others, have been reopened.

The late 1960s and the '70s saw a general decline in the level of use of the valleys service, including that to Barry.

To my amazement, the line from Barry to Barry Island was singled in 1969, as it was now used only by a depleted interval service, all excursion traffic having discontinued. Far greater use was now being made of car transport between Barry and Cardiff or bus to the excellent bus station in Central Square, approached from Wood Street. Attempts were made to save money, some involving terminating evening services from Merthyr at Cardiff General instead of running them on to Barry, thus creating an hour's wait between services at 41mins past, many passengers then making the journey by bus. With other cuts in the Valleys, this situation lasted until the mid-1980s, when John Davies, Manager for Wales, produced a plan to radically improve the Valleys service in recognition of the amount of criticism of the poor service now available and the fact there was now a specific management structure called Provincial Services in charge. With three terminal points in the valleys – Treherbert, Merthyr and Bargoed (Rhymney) – he produced a plan for a 20min. regular interval service through to Barry Island, but with mainly two-car sets, using the new Class 150 Sprinter (147 seats) and 143 Pacer (121 seats) diesel units in place of the previous three-car sets with 262 seats.

The passenger service is now in the hands of Class 150 Sprinters and Class 143 Pacers, with two-car sets unable to provide much comfort in the peak hours. Here, Pacer 143610 runs into Barry Dock with a down service when operated by Regional Railways, on 5 February 1993.

Sprinter 150230 departs Barry with a service to the Valleys and passes the now demolished Barry signal box.

This recognised the growing problems of car parking in the city of Cardiff, and the apparent regeneration of local rail travel with people commuting longer distances to work, especially in Cardiff, and the residential developments in the Vale. Soon the service would be extended by the re-opened Aberdare to Abercynon, Bridgend to Maesteg and Vale of Glamorgan services and with increasing passenger numbers travelling, a need for an increase in resources to match ensued. With privatisation, the service has now been franchised to Arriva Trains Wales, who are having to increase the length of trains to four cars (Pacers) on many Rhymney Valley trains and some elsewhere. Services to Barry Island – where the station is now merely a single short platform – are restored to a level even better than in the 1953 service days, though almost all trains are only two-car with heavy overcrowding problems on several services in the peak, creating unpleasant travelling conditions.

It is to be hoped that under plans for electrification, rolling stock will be replaced from the current outdated diesel units to new electric units, and attention focussed on realigning the track where heavy speed restrictions are still in force from steam days, so that perhaps we shall see the journey from Barry to Cardiff taking only twenty minutes.

Branch Line Services

IN ADDITION TO the main trunk route from Barry Station to Cogan and then to Cardiff, the Barry Railway had three branches, though the line to Trehafod was actually termed their main line, due to the amount of coal traffic it handled. The Barry Island branch was opened with huge success through to Barry Pier in 1896, and the station there had to be extended in 1929 due to the volume of traffic to be handled.

The layout of Gladstone Sidings between Cadoxton Low Level and Barry Dock has now been recovered and is now a road but there is still a line into/out of No. 2 Dock and a connection into the up line just west of the station which is now used to turn steam engines from Cardiff on special workings. This view is from 1993.

Barry Island Station in pre-Grouping days, then a two platform station. The view is looking west, towards Barry.

The sidings at Barry Island East seen from the signal box. The DMU fuelling point is in the centre and 5626 waits with the empty stock for a return excursion.

Barry Island East SB with Platform No. 2, previously known as the Excursion platform. 4151 is on a return excursion and the DMU Fuelling Point is centre right, the view being on 24 August 1962. Milepost 92½.

A view from underneath the station canopy on the Island platform Nos. 3 and 4, looking west. The importance of the platform awning was considerable as the coastal location made it prone to bursts of rain and wind. R.K. Blencowe Collection.

A view of Barry Pier and Harbour in Barry Railway days with a train of four wheelers at both platforms and what is probably a **J Class running** round. Two paddle steamers are in the harbour, with the Gwalia at the jetty. A ship is in Barry roads ready to enter the dock. R.K.Blencowe Collection.

A view of the former signal box and east end of the tunnel on 15 July 1957.

Ebbw Junction's 9490 leaves the tunnel with a boat connection for Newport on 16 July 1957.

An SLS Special formed of an auto set with Cathays 5574 at the Pier platform on 13 July 1957, carrying a C Special Auto target. Hugh Davies

Barry Pier in Barry Railway days.

The track out to the lighthouse on the Breakwater line. Originally two tracks, this was reduced to a single line and was closed in 1929 when the Barry Pier SB closed.

Just a single line suffices with DMU operation, as a six-car set makes a boat connection in the 1960s.
T.J. Edgington.

The **Vale of Glamorgan** branch opened in 1896, the prime object being to attract Tondu Valley coal to Barry Docks. This the Barry Company never succeeded in doing to their full desires and the line never achieved its full potential. Its passenger service thrived in the morning and evening peak hours and during the summer and at weekends, but other than at those times, carryings were relatively light from the 1920s onward. Stations were provided at Rhoose, Aberthaw, Gileston, St.Athan, Llantwit Major, Llandow (Wick Road) Halt, Llandow Halt and Southerndown Road.

Planned weekend engineering work on the main line resulted in regular diversion of all main line traffic between Cardiff and Bridgend via Barry and the Vale, and this continues to this day. Several industrial concerns developed along the line, Rhoose and Aberthaw Cement Works and Aberthaw A and then B Power Stations, and finally the Ford Motor Company at Cowbridge Road. The passenger service was removed under the Beeching cuts of 1964, but it must have been a flimsy case for closure as the line still had to be maintained to full passenger standards for diversions and coal traffic still passing to Aberthaw. Most travel was to and from Rhoose and Llantwit Major with little beyond, Cardiff passengers for Bridgend travelling via the main line.

The Vale of Glamorgan service in 1924 showed only eight services, plus the Ports to Ports which ran non-stop between Barry and Bridgend. The services were:

5.55am Barry-Llantwit 8am Barry-Bridgend (7.35am ex-Riverside)
10.10am Barry to Bridgend 12.40pm Barry-Bridgend
1.40pm WSO Barry-Llantwit 2.55pm Barry-Bridgend
5.15pm Barry-Llantwit 9.25pm Barry to Llanwit SX 10.30pm SO

There was thus no train beyond Llantwit Major from 3.41pm (2.55pm ex-Barry) until next day.

Porthkerry Viaduct as seen from the road into Rhoose.

During the 1930s, services on the Cardiff-Barry-Vale of Glamorgan line were worked by Barry, Canton and Cathays depots. Canton used H targets and here their TV Class A 335 is on turn HA, an auto service with a non-auto fitted engine, running through Porthkerry Park with what is probably a train for Llantwit Major in 1936.

Cathays TV Class A 364 with an up six-coach train which may be through from Bridgend approaching Porthkerry Tunnel in 1936.

Barry's A Class 404 which became 306 in 1948 rounds a tight bend in Porthkerry Park with a down target BD service to either Llantwit Major or Bridgend in 1936.

Barry's 361 heads a down train in Porthkerry Park also with the BD target. Notice the fact that some engines are running engine first in the down direction.

Barry's 372 is working turn BM on this down train probably to Llantwit Major in 1936.

Barry turn BE heads west to Bridgend behind Barry's 5699.

In this pastoral scene, a 56XX heads east with an up service seen from the western portal of Porthkerry Tunnel also in 1936.

The 10.8am Barry to Llantwit Major leaves Barry and passes under Ship Hill bridge behind Barry's 5195, which was transferred to Treherbert for the start of the Regular Interval service in September 1953.

With the introduction of the Regular Interval service in 1953, Barry, Cathays and Tondu were allocated auto-fitted 4575 Class engines to replace the 64XX previously used, though Barry did not have any of these. Here Barry's new 5529 on turn BA heads a Barry to Llantwit Major auto after working the 5.15am Barry to Pontypridd auto, return to Clarence Road, thence back to Barry.

Leaving Barry with the 5.43pm Clarence Road to Bridgend, 5613 steams under Ship Hill bridge with its five-coach train.

Having just left Porthkerry Tunnel, 5687 climbs the bank with a Sunday Queen Street to Llantwit Major service, target CC.

82007 runs through Porthkerry Park with a Barry to Llantwit Major train in 1954.

82035 passes under Ship Hill bridge with a Barry to Llanwit Major service, target BE and passes a TV Class A on the Up Relief line.

A Radyr 56XX on turn C09, running through from a Valleys colliery to Aberthaw Power Station pulls out of Barry Sidings where a 72XX banker has been attached for the climb up Porthkerry bank in 1964. Ian L. Wright.

6614 heads the 5.43pm Clarence Road to Bridgend past Barry Sidings where 6754 awaits any banking duties on 5 July 1957.

A down evening freight heads through Porthkerry Park hauled by a 7200 Class engine, converted from a 52XX, the picture taken in the late 1930s.

7214 heads a down mixed freight through Porthkerry Park also in the late 1930s.

One of the last 52XXs with a down mixed freight in Porthkerry Park in the late 1930s.

The summer service for 1959 provided eighteen services SX plus four more SO between Barry and Llantwit Major, of which six continued to Bridgend. By the winter of 1963-64, this had been reduced to ten services to Llantwit Major with three continuing to Bridgend, trains running mostly in the peak hours, with a four hour gap in the morning from 8.13am to 12.15pm, and a three hour gap in the evening from 6.37pm to 9.25pm. The Sunday service provided in 1959 had gone by 1963-4.

I travelled on the last train from Barry to Llantwit Major, the 9.25pm on the day of closure in June 1964, returning at 10pm with the last up train. This was at a time when local passenger travel found bus travel cheaper and more frequent than rail. The later 1960s and '70s were lean times for the Cardiff Valleys service, with cuts made which destroyed the regular interval pattern and created hourly intervals where a train every 30mins had been the norm. The service was still worth keeping but what was happening on the roads would, during the 1990s, create a need for an alternative to be exploited to tackle the gridlock conditions on the approaches to Cardiff and the problems of car parking in the city, especially at peak hours. A case was first made to reopen a line into the Tondu Valleys, closed in 1970, as far as Maesteg and this was followed by a case for the reopening of the Vale of Glamorgan, with just the two most important stations restored at Rhoose and Llantwit Major, where there had been major housing developments in the intervening years providing a considerable need for an improvement on the road service to Cardiff. A connecting bus service was and still is provided from Rhoose station to Cardiff International Airport, but the small number of passengers it conveys makes one wonder why a locally sponsored taxi service could not cope.

The new Vale of Glamorgan service opened in 2005 with an hourly service between Cardiff Central and Bridgend, and has been such a success, particularly in the peak hours, that there is now a case to improve the service to half-hourly if only in the peaks. There are also calls for additional stations to be provided. The 0742 service from Bridgend leaves Rhoose (0806) full and anyone joining at Barry and beyond has to stand.

The **Cadoxton to Pontypridd/Porth (via Wenvoe)** line was originally termed the Barry Railway main line service from Barry to Trehafod (freight) and Porth (passenger), but this was almost completely overtaken by the Barry-Cardiff-Rhondda service, especially following the introduction of the regular interval service in September 1953 which provided through services. The line was essentially created for coal traffic from the Rhondda Valley to Barry Docks and even in Barry Railway days was little used for normal passenger traffic, the only intermediate stations being at Wenvoe, Creigiau and Efail Isaf. Even the 1923 timetable showed only five trains a day:

4.44am SO/5.35am SX Barry to Porth (Not Calling at Wenvoe)
7.58am Barry to Porth 12.27pm, 4.55pm
7.08pm Barry Island to Porth

Additionally, there was the former Barry Railway service from Cardiff Riverside to Pontypridd via Ely and St.Fagans which joined the line at Tynycaeau Junction with seven trains a day at 9.07am, 12.50pm, 3.05pm, 5.22pm, 6.40pm, 8.45pm. and 10.45pm.

By 1953, the service from Cardiff had been reduced to three trains at 8.38am, 12.50pm and 5.38pm, with three services on the Cadoxton line also, all provided by a Railmotor. From 1958 the service was reduced to office hour times with a 7.45am Barry to Pontypridd and another service from Cadoxton around 5pm, with return trains to and from Cardiff General (Pl.8/9) at 12.50 and 5.36pm, worked by Abercynon Turn JB with a 64XX, previously a 35XX Metro tank, and subsequently a 2Car DMU.

Wenvoe Station on 6 August 1957 as Barry's 5527 runs in with the 4.55pm auto from Barry to Pontypridd.
Ian L. Wright.

A Barry Railway scene at Creigiau in pre-Grouping days as a train from Barry to either Pontypridd or Port runs in.

The layout at Wenvoe as recorded on 2 June 1953. R.C. Riley.

The 5.31pm Clarence Road to Pontypridd was a long standing service in later years and is seen here standing under the footbridge at Creigiau worked by Abercynon turn JB with engine 6438 9 September 1960.
S. Rickard/J&J Collection.

A down shipment coal train from Abercynon to Cadoxton, probably emanating from Lady Windsor colliery, passes Efail Isaf behind Abercynon's 5641, running as X13 on 15 July 1959. H.C. Casserley.

Use of the sidings in Cadoxton Yard declined during the late 1950s as can be seen here as Treherbert's 5607 runs through the yard with a relief service from Treherbert to Barry Island in 9 June 1957.

Part of the yard can be seen in this shot of a return train to Aberdare from Barry Island behind Aberdare's 6651 in the late 1950s.

The essentially coal traffic line from the Rhondda, Merthyr and Rhymney Valleys to Barry Dock for shipment was heavily used on weekends and Bank Holidays by excursion traffic to Barry Island. The line was closed in 1963 when it was found that all the remaining coal trains could be easily catered for on the Pontypridd-Radyr line. By this time, shipment traffic, though concentrated at Barry Docks from Newport and Cardiff Docks was very much in decline as was the day-tripper traffic to Barry Island.

Drope Junction as a down train of empty stock for Barry Island passes behind 5615 on 6 August 1957.
Ian L. Wright.

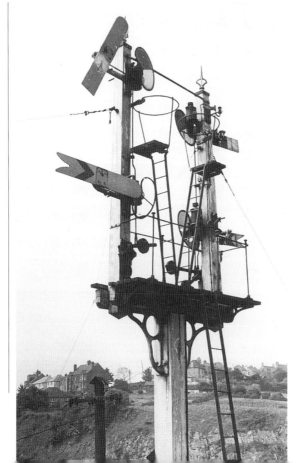

This fine former Barry Railway set of up and down bracket somersault signals was in the centre of the yard and was Cadoxton North's home signal, seen on 14 June 1959.

CHAPTER 7

COAL & FREIGHT TRAFFIC

BARRY OWES ITS very existence to coal traffic by rail and until the Grouping in 1922 this was worked into the area by the Barry Company's own engines and crews. Details of the rise and fall of this traffic were given under the Docks section, but comments here centre on the railway accommodation for the traffic and the actual services. For traffic coming down the 'main line' from Trehafod into Cadoxton, a large reception and storage yard of thirty-seven sidings was built at Cadoxton (also known as Palmerston). The running lines ran through the middle of the yard with eighteen sidings on the down side for loaded traffic and nineteen on the up side for empties. From here, traffic was called forward for individual vessels at their berths with nominated engines of the Barry fleet used to work trains of up to a hundred loaded wagons on the flat, first to other holding sidings for No. 1 Dock located between Barry Dock station and Barry Engine Works from where wagons were placed on the

tip roads leading to the coal hoists from where they were discharged into the waiting vessels. With the opening of No. 2 Dock in 1896, a second set of holding sidings was created between Barry Dock station and Cadoxton, consisting of twenty-four sidings, through which ran two running lines, the more northerly dividing the yard into two, the sidings between there and the main line used as a general traffic yard and the through running lines on the south side feeding the tip roads and acting as through lines between Cadoxton Yard and the holding yard for No. 1 Dock, which the other set of through lines duplicated. In addition to these yards, at Cadoxton there were other holding sidings alongside the Cogan main line. Coal traffic arriving from the Cogan direction, mainly from the Newport Valleys, was normally held in the sidings between Cadoxton and Barry Dock, which were generally known as Barry Dock Storage Sidings, those at the east end also known as Gladstone Sidings.

Cadoxton Yard used for the storage of loaded shipment coal which was then called forward for loading into waiting vessels, and the return of empties to the collieries after unloading. Trains of up to 100 wagons ran from here to the holding sidings at Barry Dock from where the wagons were placed in rafts onto the tip roads.

This is the view from the bedroom window of our house in Dock View Road and shows Barry Dock Storage Sidings running between Barry Dock and Cadoxton stations, with the low-level lines into the Docks by tunnel and the main line out of sight in the foreground. There were twenty-four sidings with two control boxes, with the six sidings next the lines into the Docks worked as a separate yard from the other eighteen sidings used exclusively for shipment coal.

A view across the six sidings nearest the low level lines into the Dock showing the control cabin with a Type 3 diesel running in with a mixed freight from Cardiff in 1964.

Another view from our bedroom window showing the Storage Sidings with condemned coaches, vans and 43XX engines in the yard. Both control boxes can be seen in this view. There is little in the way of shipment coal in this 1964 shot, even though all bituminous shipment coal from South East Wales was concentrated at Barry Docks since 1963.

A mixed freight arrives into the Storage Sidings yard behind a Type 3 diesel in 1964.

A view of the west end of the Storage Sidings serving No. 2 Dock coal hoists with Barry's 9451 on shunting duties. At the end of the 1940s, there were up to seven shunting engines engaged at these sidings, a mixture of Barry Railway B1s and 67XXs, when shunting activities continued over twenty-four hours.

6637 on turn B9 crosses from the up relief to the up main at Barry Junction with an up train of empty minerals on 24 January 1953.

389 brings another train of empty minerals past Barry Station on 24 January 1953.

389 waits the road to cross the junction at Ship Hill bridge in 1950 with two wagons of livestock for unloading at the jetty in Barry station yard. The engine had just been overhauled in Barry Works during May and June and was now fresh out of shops.

215 passes Barry
Docks station with
turn C2 tripping
a load of empty
minerals off the tips
via the High Level
Sidings to Cadoxton
Yard on 25 April
1953.

At the Grouping there were thirty coal service targets in use from Cadoxton Yard to the Interchange Yard with other Railways, engines leaving Barry shed fifteen minutes in advance of the starting time from Cadoxton Yard, and first picking up a brakevan at Barry Van Sidings alongside the shed. The target letter for Barry at that time was By, but later became simply B. Details of services were:

By. 2 3.15am to Trehafod or Treforest Junction
By. 3 4.15am to Penrhos Junction
By. 5 5.00am to Duffryn Isaf (B&M)
By. 6 5.15am to Peterston Junction
By. 8 6.15am to Duffryn Isaf (B&M)
By.10 7.15am to Penrhos Junction
By.11 7.45am to Trehafod or Treforest Junction
By.12 8.45am to Duffryn Isaf (B&M)
By.14 9.25am to Trehafod or Treforest Junction
By.15 10.30am to Penrhos Junction
By.16 10.45am to Trehafod or Treforest Junction

By.17 11.00am to Peterston Junction
By.18 11.15am to Duffryn Isaf (B&M)
By.19 11.50am to Penrhos
By.21 1.25pm to Peterston Junction
By.22 10am Barry to Trehafod
By.23 1.45pm to Trehafod or Treforest Junction
By.25 3.05pm to Trehafod or Treforest Junction
By.26 3.45pm to Duffryn Isaf (B&M)
By.27 4.45pm to Penrhos Junction
By.28 5.15pm to Duffryn Isaf (B&M)
By.31 6.25pm to Trehafod or Treforest Junction
By.32 6.55pm to Peterston Junction
By.34 7.20pm to Penrhos Junction
By.35 8.00pm to Trehafod or Treforest Junction
By.37 9.00pm to Trehafod or Treforest Junction
By.38 9.25pm to Peterston Junction
By.39 9.35pm to Penrhos Junction
By.42 10.30pm to Trehafod or Treforest Junction
By.44 11.45pm to Trehafod ot Treforest Junction

The destination of trains was under the direction of the Controller at Barry Docks, located in the Barry Railway Offices:

Coal from Trehafod was from collieries in the Rhondda Fawr or Fach.

Treforest Junction was from collieries in the Merthyr & Aberdare areas.

Penrhos Junction was from collieries in the Rhymney Valley.

Peterston Junction was from collieries in the Tondu & Llantrisant Valleys.

Duffryn Isaf was from collieries on the Brecon & Merthyr Railway.

In Barry Railway days of maximum coal movement, all the By.Target Nos. would have been used from By.1 to By.44.

Wagons for coal traffic were originally provided by the colliery companies, with a huge variety of names on view across the sidings, often abbreviated to starting letters, e.g. SC (Stephenson Clarke), GLM (Glamorgan Collieries) etc. Inward loaded trains from collieries would be composed of all wagons bearing that colliery name. These had to be returned in the same way, so that before trains could depart, they also had to be composed of serviceable wagons bearing just that colliery's name. As coal from different collieries could be blended on the tip roads, large amounts of shunting was often involved, while this was also occasioned by wagons becoming damaged and needing repair before they could be returned. Overall, there was a twenty-four hour operation between these holding sidings with up to seven shunting engines employed at the key yard between Cadoxton and Barry Dock stations.

With the huge railway workload during the Second World War, it was decided in 1942 that coal wagons could become common user in an effort to reduce the vast amount of shunting necessary. Though this facility became available, it was not widely practised in the area and the heavy shunting continued until Nationalisation in 1948, when the railway began to provide the wagons

for coal traffic in the form of new steel bodied 16ton unbranded which became widespread during the 1950s. These were in addition to the 20ton steel bodied wagons which had been introduced from the 1920s by the then General Manager Felix Pole, but which soon became used largely for loco coal, as some collieries and coal hoists were unable to take the larger wagons. 16ton non-vacuum fitted wagons became the norm for shipment coal during the 1950s, though they were fitted with an end door only at one end. Shunters were encouraged to ensure all wagons were supplied the right way round, though most coal hoists had a turntable where wagons could be turned before tipping. The wooden coal wagon was phased out during the late 1950s though with many examples surviving into the 1960s.

Export coal traffic began to decline after the First World War as ships changed from coal to oil firing. This had a considerable effect on the level of business at Barry Docks from which it did not really recover. One benefit was the emergence of power station coal by coastwise shipping with Barry Docks always hosting several such small boats used to supply South Wales coal to power stations such as Battersea which lay alongside rivers. There were several of these fleets, the Power boats and the Fulham boats being two of the most prolific. With the decline in the use of coal for steam engines, house heating etc. during the 1960s, the amount of shipment coal passing through the South Wales ports saw a considerable decrease and in 1963, the Docks Board decided to concentrate all bituminous coal shipment at Barry and all anthracite at Swansea, meaning an end to coal shipment at both Newport and Cardiff, where more space was needed for general cargo anyway, and of which Barry had very little. The pace of decline in the shipment market however defeated this initiative and by the end of the 1960s, very little continued

Geest banana traffic from the West Indies began at Barry Docks in 1959 and lasted until the mid-1960s when it moved to Southampton. This labour-intensive scene shows wagons being loaded from the boat which arrived on Sunday evening where the west end of the north side of No. 2 was reserved for this traffic.

to exist. The 1970s saw a resurgence in coke traffic by sea and a mechanised coke loader was built on the north side of No. 2 Dock, dealing with coke from Nantgarw and Cwm but its lifespan was short and it soon became redundant, marking the end of coal and coke shipment traffic through Barry.

With the change to imported coal, especially low volatile coal for power stations, Barry saw a few cargoes of such traffic for power stations, mostly Didcot, and these were handled by the high capacity cranes at the east end of No. 2 Dock, but this traffic was better handled at either Newport or Avonmouth from where the rail journey was shorter, and Barry's association with coal now became consigned to history, representing a complete turn of the wheel in the century from the 1880s which had given rise to its existence.

As mentioned earlier, the end of the 1950s saw a new traffic arrive at Barry Docks in the form of Geest banana traffic from the West Indies, with one or sometimes two boats arriving on Sunday afternoons. Unloading began at once and often the first train of ventilated vans was ready for despatch that evening. Dependent on the tonnage conveyed per boat, trains ran to distribution centres throughout England on Monday to Wednesday with trains treated by the WR as specials for which engines had to be found by Control. A Banana Train Controller (Mike Phillips) was provided in the Divisional Control Office who arranged services, wagons, power and crews. Banana boats were dealt with at the west end of No. 2 dock on the south side where the bananas were loaded to vans for despatch, keeping a 67XX continuously occupied.

There were three services a day provided as specials from Cadoxton to London, Crewe and other places as ordered and here Standard Class 5 No. 73026 sets off from Cadoxton with the 7.10pm to Crewe in the early 1960s.

Another view of the 7.10pm banana special to Crewe leaving Cadoxton behind Shrewsbury Jubilee 45651 Shovell in 1963.

The evening 6.30pm Cardiff Newtown to Llandilo Junction via Barry passes Barry Dock with the Dock Offices in the background and 4225 at the head.

Trainloads per destination were taken from the dockside to Cadoxton Low Level Sidings from where trains to a variety of places were run, normally three or four trains per day, engines sent from Canton to Barry Shed and trains then worked by Barry traincrews through to Gloucester, Hereford and Bristol, the extent of their route knowledge, and enabling them to return in a day's turn. Trains ran through to Acton, Crewe and other centres, and brought some very interesting and unique engine working to Barry, including two Royal Scots and several Jubilees for the Crewe service, with many unbalanced Castles used for the London services.

Another new traffic developed in the early 1960s was bulk cargoes of iron ore, manganese ore, phosphate rock and imported coal, unloaded by grab-crane at the east end of No. 2 Dock on the north side, beyond the former No. 26 coal hoist. All this traffic in either hoppers or sheeted 16ton mineral wagons ran in block trains mostly to the Midlands on a specials basis, and lasted until the mid-1960s.

General cargo traffic always produced a wide variety of freight traffic, especially timber, including much pitprop traffic for the Valleys collieries, oil traffic from the storage tanks at the west end of No. 1 Dock, flour traffic from Rank's Mill on No. 2 Dock and chemical traffic to and from Dow Corning at the east end of No. 2 Dock.

Running through Barry, coal traffic has passed to Aberthaw Power Station since the early 1960s, first to the A station and then to the much larger B station. Initially, traffic for the A station was staged at Barry Dock Storage Sidings between Cadoxton and Barry Dock, portions arriving which were formed into complete trains, though with some through trains. Trains were double headed by two 5600 Class 0-6-2Ts throughout to Aberthaw to negotiate Porhtkerry bank, and made an impressive sight as they accelerated away after leaving Barry Dock. With the opening of the B station, this was fed by MGR services and coincided with the introduction of diesel engines, Class 37s being used, either singly or two in multiple, or even three for a while. These were replaced by Class 60 diesels and later by Class 66 with 100 ton hopper wagons in trains of 3000 tons.

Emerging from the tunnel under Barry Dock Storage Sidings from No. 2 Dock, Stanier 8F 48412 heads a train of imported phosphate rock conveyed in sheeted 16tonners to Oldbury in the early 1960s. It was very unusual for a main line engine to work a train from the dock, the normal starting point being Cadoxton Low Level.

A view taken from the clock tower at the former Dock Offices of a Class 37 running through Barry Docks station with a Tower to Aberthaw MGR train in the 1990s. There are just two lines left in the former Storage Sidings but they will soon disappear and the whole complex will become a road.

In the early 1960s, coal for Aberthaw A Power Station was staged through Barry Dock Storage Sidings from where trains were double headed to Aberthaw. Here 6655 and 5685 start the train past Barry Dock station on 18th February 1961.

6619 and 6655 work the 10.30am train past Gladstone Bridge between Barry Docks and Barry stations on 16 March 1961.

To increase the MGR load, the Class 37s were used in multiple as here in this picture at Barry station taken from the footbridge in the late 1960s.

The whole of the former Storage Sidings has now been removed and is being converted into a road. A Class 56 works the evening chemicals train to Blackpool out of No. 2 Dock in the 1990s.

A double-headed MGR with Class 37 37899 and another in charge run across Porthkerry Viaduct with a train from Cwmbargoed to Aberthaw B in the 1990s.

Two Class 37s in multiple head a train of MGR wagons to Aberthaw B passing under Ship Hill Bridge. The Up Relief line was taken out in May 1964 when Barry Sidings Yard was closed, leaving just a Down Goods Loop line.

Towards the end of the century these were replaced by 100ton hoppers in trains of over 2,000 tons, worked first by Class 60s and now by Class 66s. Much coal has often been worked through Cwmbargoed, and the present day sees large amounts from the new opencast site at Ffos y Fran worked that way. Coal from sites west of Aberthaw has always featured, including from Blaenant over many years, Cwmgwrach, Wern Tarw etc., running via Bridgend and through the west end connections into Aberthaw Reception Sidings.

Cement traffic has long passed from Aberthaw Cement Works and more recently oil traffic in first 45 and now 100ton tankers. There is now a new flow of cement traffic from the Aberthaw Works to Moorswater and Westbury with three full trains per week with return empties, hauled by the new Class 70 locos. The Vale line also sees traffic to and from the Ford plant at Bridgend which is served off a Cowbridge Road connection.

The changing face of freight traffic on the Barry line from the 1930s to the 1990s. (Top) A new 5228 accelerates up Porthkerry bank with a down freight in the mid-1930s, the first truck a 10ton wooden wagon, while (Bottom) Class 56 56113 draws an empty MGR train out of the former Gladstone Sidings at Cadoxton in 1994. The 32ton MGR wagons have now been overtaken by 100ton hoppers.

CHAPTER 8

BARRY ENGINE SHED & WORKS

PRIOR TO THE Grouping, each of the private companies in South Wales had their own principal depot or works to repair and maintain their locomotive fleet. Barry engine shed was a substantial depot, with a 6 road shed, in which engines could be prepared for their next turn of duty, a turntable which could be used to turn their 0-8-0 engines, or indeed any other engine, facilities to carry out running repairs, including those involving lifting, and the usual depot facilities such as a coaling stage and a large yard at the back of the shed. The capability of the depot was to carry out any repair below main works level, with the ability to pass such engines onto Barry Works, or as it was known Barry Factory. The turntable ceased to be required on a daily basis after the 0-8-0 engines had been withdrawn and was removed in April 1953.

At the Grouping, there were 130 engines allocated to Barry, which represented the whole of the Barry Railway fleet other than those allocated to Trehafod, and included six GWR engines, three of the 3100 Class and three of the 4200 Class, on loan or hired to assist with the Barry availability situation. There were twelve engines allocated to Trehafod, which included one of the D Class 0-8-0s (1387), most being of the B and B1 Classes.

By 1930, the allocation had been reduced to 113. Considerable inroads had been made into the Barry fleet (as set out in Chapter 4). There were still forty of the B and B1 Classes in use on freight work, but passenger duties were now in the hands of fourteen former TV Class As which had been joined by four of the 3900 Class, though three of these would be condemned in the autumn. There were still six of the F Class on shunting duties with three of the E Class. At the start of the year there were still three of the J Class 2-4-2Ts engaged on passenger duties but all were withdrawn by May. Three of the H Class 0-8-2Ts heavy freight were still working in January but all, plus the last 0-8-0 (1390), had gone by August. Of the 4200 Class sent to Barry to bridge the gap until the arrival of the 5600 Class, there were still sixteen allocated but the 5600 Class allocation by January 1930 stood at twenty-three, including several which were to become long-standing Barry engines until the end of their lives.

By January 1940, the allocation had been further reduced to eighty-seven, of which the seven remaining 52XXs would all go to Ebbw.Junction in March. The Barry B and B1s stood at twenty-five, with the two Es with fifteen TV Class A. Three veteran GWR panniers had been imported to help with shunting, the main thrust of which now fell to the 67XXs of which eleven were allocated. Twenty-four of the 56 and 66XXs were now allocated for coal and freight working. Three ex-Rhymney A Class (57-59) arrived during 1948 and stayed until 1951 when all were transferred to Radyr.

May1953 was the month in which I got my introduction to Barry shed, through a chance meeting with the Shedmaster Ernie Breakspear. At this time, the Barry allocation was eighty engines; the last of the Barry B1s had gone in April 1951 and the allocation was now made up sixteen former Taff Vale 0-6-2Ts and sixty-four GWR/BR(WR), almost all on shed on my first Sunday visit:-

Taff Vale O4 0-6-2T:- 210/11/15/85 (from March-September)

Taff Vale Class A 0-6-2T:- 306/12/57/61/72/73/75/82/87/88/89/94

850 Class 0-6-0T:- 2008 1600 Class:- 0-6-0T 1600/15

5101 Class 2-6-2T:- 4160/61/63/77, 5183/95

4200 Class 2-8-0T:- 4224, 4267

5600 Class 0-6-2T:- 5609/14/19/21/27/32/48/64/65/67,

6614/15/19/20/37/41/43/58/68/69

5700 Class 0-6-0T:- 4601, 4692, 5751, 6712/22/23/24/33/36/38,

6740/45/46/47/48/50/52/53/54/58/69/74/75,

7726/79, 9631/76

9400 Class 0-6-0T: 8451/58/60/61/65/69

The Taff Vale O4s were used on local tripping and shunting, the depot's C turns.

The Taff Vale A Class were used on passenger services on the Cardiff, Vale of Glamorgan and Pontypridd (BR) routes. They also worked coal services.

The 850 and 1600 Classes were used on dock shunting. the 850 especially on the Goods shed pilot.

The 4200 Class were mostly used on banking turns such as the Porthkerry banker and on Rogerstone services.

The 5101 Class were used exclusively on passenger services on the Cardiff and Vale of Glamorgan routes.

The 5600 Class were used on freight and coal services, working the Barry B turns.

The 5700 and 9400 Class were used on shunting and tripping, the depot's P turns.

372 in a posed picture possibly outside the Carriage Shed in the early 1930s. It had been rebuilt at Swindon in 1926 which is evidenced by the straight topped side tanks, the round topped ones being modified at Caerphilly.

The west end of Barry shed in the 1940s with TV Class A 389 leading, a Rhymney A either 57, 58 or 59 and two Barry B or B1 Class at the rear.

After the Grouping, Barry always had several of the Taff Vale 04s, which were employed on secondary work of tripping and shunting as opposed to the Class As which did passenger work until 1953. Here 211 stands in the yard on 17 May 1953.

285 was another of several O4s at Barry and is seen in the yard on 16 August 1953.

Barry had a dozen or so TV Class As, including 349 which was previously a Pontypool Road engine (with 385) and often used as a Llanvihangel banker.

361 standing with now preserved 6619 at the back of the shed in 1953.

For work around the dock, including shunting the Goods Yard, Barry had two of the small 850 Class, Nos. 1993 and 2008. Here 2008 stands in the yard on 3 May 1953.

Prior to the start of the Cardiff Valleys Regular Interval Service in September 1953, Barry had six of the excellent large Prairie tanks, the 5101 Class, though most were in the 41XX series. After 1953, their presence on the shed was mainly off incoming excursions as here with Radyr's 4126, lined out in green after a visit to Caerphilly Works in 1957, and standing against the shed wall in Summer 1958.

Barry's now preserved 4160 (now to be seen on the West Somerset Railway) stands at the front of the shed in early 1953, before transfer to Rhymney.

Though Barry had an allocation of some two dozen of the 4200 Class in the years after the Grouping, this was gradually reduced until in the 1940s and 50s there were usually only two, though also with two of the 72xxs, one of their uses being on banking coal trains to Aberthaw Power Station up Porthkerry bank, the others being on coal trains from the Valleys. Here 4278 stands next to a 72XX at the back of the shed in the late 1950s.

It was common to see a 4300 Class Mogul on shed on the weekend in Summer as most excursions from Gloucester and Cheltenham were worked by this class, which, having deposited the empty stock in the High Level sidings, could be turned on the west end of No. 1 Dock, so the crew could spend the rest of the day at Barry instead of having to return to Canton as all 4-6-0s were constrained to do. Here Gloucester's 5398 stands on the ash road where she will be chalked up for coal and fire attention ready for the evening return.

The 5600 Class were normally present on Barry shed in large numbers, either home based or incoming on excursion work at weekends in summer. Here Barry's now preserved 6619 stands at the front of the shed awaiting its next duty.

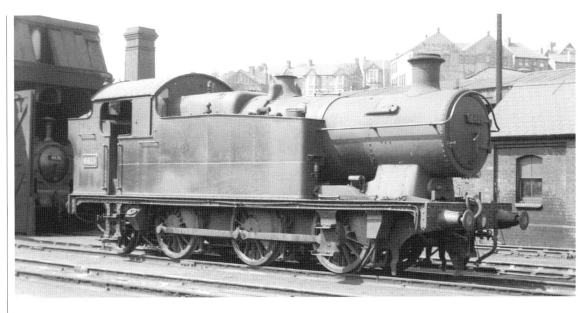

Seven of the 5600 Class line up on the ash road off incoming excursions from the Valleys in June 1959, headed by 6652 of Aberdare. They would normally run south bunker first and return engine first.

There were normally a batch of the 5700 Class panniers allocated to Barry, but not many of the original 57XX series, the exception being 5769 in the mid to late 1950s, here seen from the coal stage on 28 April 1957.

Barry's allocation of panniers was mainly for dock and yard shunting in the form of the 67XX series. Long term resident 6746 is seen in the yard in 1958.

One of the pair of 7200 Class normally allocated to Barry in the late 1950s, 7241 is seen recently ex-Caerphilly Works at the shed in summer 1958.

For the start of the Cardiff Valleys Regular Interval service in September 1953, a fleet of 10 Standard Class 3 2-6-2Ts were transferred to Barry from the Birmingham area. For crew training on the class, 82000 was based at Barry from the beginning of August and is seen at the shed alongside TV Class A 394, which they replaced on passenger work, on 9 August 1953.

The original batch of 82000-09 were replaced by batch of new engines 83036-44 which had larger coal bunkers and here 82036 heads a line-up of the class at the front of the shed on Sunday 27 May 1956, ready for their Monday morning duties.

The Tredegar based ex-LNW 0-8-0 was a regular Sunday and Bank Holiday visitor to Barry on the Nantybwch excursion which had been running since the early years of the century. The most regular performer on the working was 49064 seen on 31 July 1955 after turning on the dock, the layout suitable because of the flangeless wheel. 5644 is alongside off an excursion from Aberdare.

An interesting sight during the late 1950s was this ex-Barry Railway 4 wheeler which was still in use as part of the Barry breakdown set and is seen at the shed in summer 1958.

Prior to the introduction of the Regular Interval Passenger service in September 1953, almost all the services on the Barry to Cardiff service were worked by Barry turns, carrying B targets, e.g. BA, BB, BC etc., hauled by Taff Vale Class As, 5101 Class (of the 41XX series) or 5600 Class.

The main freight and coal services carried B targets followed by a number between B5 and B43, split mostly between the 5600 Class and the Taff Vale Class As, as follows:

5600 Class:- B5, B6, B7, B9, B13, B20, B21, B26, B29, B32, B39, B40, B42; these were the heaviest coal train services from Valleys collieries and yards to Barry Docks.

Taff Vale Class A:- B10, B16, B24, B25 (passed to 56XX from end 1953), B30, B31, B36 and B43: these were lighter freight services, though could be powered on occasions by a 56XX if the loads were known to be heavier. From September 1953, the TV Class A's ceased to work passenger services which passed to the Standard Class 3 82XXXs and were used on the lighter freight and coal services.

9400 Class:- B15, B34 4200 Class B41 (Porthkerry Banker); there were nine C targets which brought traffic from Cadoxton Yard to the tips and returned empties, these being in the range C2 to C11, C1 and C9 missing, though were doubtless there in the earlier years. These turns were split between Taff Vale Class As and 67XX in 1953/4.

There were thirteen P targets which were Pilot shunting turns in the marshalling yards and on the docks. P11 was a docks turn, always worked by a 16XX. In 1953/4 the turns were numbered P1-16 and would have been 16 turns in the earlier days.

There were three other turns at the depot, target BD1, a docks turn worked by a 16XX, the Factory Pilot (FAC.P.) worked by a 67XX or an ex-works 0-6-0T, which worked engines from the shed to the Works and vice versa with any associated wagons and undertook any engine movements on the shed, and the Llantwit Major Pilot (LLWT.PILOT) which shunted Llantwit Major Yard and undertook any movements of wagons in that area of the Vale.

In my archive, I have full details of the engines allocated to each of the Barry freight turns from December 1953 to April 1954.

For the start of the Regular Interval service in September 1953, 10 Standard Class 3 2-6-2Ts were allocated from Tyseley and these were subsequently replaced by ten of the new builds from Swindon in the series 82032-44 with larger coal bunkers, two of which were supplied daily to Merthyr for their MA and MC turns.

Barry Engine Works opened shortly after the setting up of the company for the repair and modification of engines belonging to the Barry Company. New engines were always bought in from established manufacturers and were never built at the works. Following the Grouping of 1922, the GWR used Barry Works as an addition to their own and their inherited engine works, and as an alternative in South Wales to the main works at Caerphilly. The layout at the two works could hardly have been more different, the newly-designed Caerphilly being laid out along the lines of A Shop at Swindon but Barry simply having engines placed one behind the other on three tracks with restricted clearance between. For this reason, engines with outside cylinders could not easily be handled due to the problems they created with clearance, though the odd few were handled from time to time.

Engines from all parts of South Wales were sent to Barry Works from 1922, and this was extended by the GWR Shopping Control to engines from any part of the system, even a pannier from Swindon in the 1950s. Two engines that stand out in my memory were 2183 from Croes Newydd, and Cambrian 0-6-0 895 for smokebox repairs for which Barry was selected over nearby Wolverhampton and Oswestry Works.

Barry Works, opened in 1887 by the Barry Railway, seen here on 13 September 1953, with 322 of Abercynon and 1445 of Hereford awaiting attention.

Another view in March 1955 with 386, 4632 and 5661 awaiting.

A view inside the works with 5600 Class engines standing on the three tracks. The narrowness of the space between the three tracks precluded outside cylinder engines being repaired. Eric Mountford.

Swansea Docks shunter 1151 ex-works in March 1953.

The 1400 Class were frequent visitors for overhaul, here 1415 of Bristol Bath Road.

2183 of Croes Newydd more likely to be sent to Wolverhampton Works, was overhauled in August and September 1954 and is seen at the shed on 25 September.

Ex-Burry Port & Gwendraeth Valley engines sometimes appeared as here with 2198 ex-works at the shed on 13 September 1955.

As they were inside cylinder, the 2251 Class were also dealt with in the latter 1950s as here with 2292 of Severn Tunnel seen outside the works on 2 December 1957.

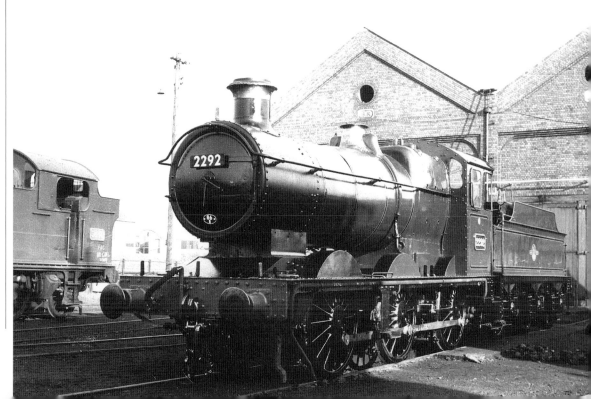

All types of repair were undertaken at Barry from a smokebox to a Heavy General or Intermediate Overhaul, after which engines were turned out freshly painted. During the 1950s, when I used to see all the engines that passed through, the main classes handled were Taff Vale Class As, 56XX, 57XX, 16XX, 14XX, BPGV and Swansea Docks Shunters. In the late 1950s, Barry also began repairing the 2251 Class inside cylinder engines which fitted their clearance requirements. Barry also undertook the modifications required to the 46XX panniers before they were transferred to the Southern.

The start of dieselisation in the late 1950s had an obvious effect on the number of works necessary and the smallest works, such as Barry, were the first to go, leaving Caerphilly to handle all the repair work in South Wales. Barry Works closed in 1959 with a final 56XX given the full treatment and turned out in lined green.

Though there were very few of the class in South East Wales, there were several of the 7400 Class based at Carmarthen for the branch line passenger and milk working to Felin Fach and Pont Llanio on the Aberayron and Newcastle Emlyn branches. Like the 5400 and 6400 Classes, the 74s had larger driving wheels but were not auto fitted. The Carmarthen engines mostly came to Barry Works for overhaul.

CHAPTER 9

EXCURSION TRAFFIC

THE PHENOMENAL SUCCESS of Barry Island as a day tripper destination began in the early years of the century with excursions run from both the Valleys and main line origins. It increased after the Grouping under GWR marketing and was still very strong in the 1950s, when the Holiday Express was re-introduced, this having first come into being in the 1930s, with Barry Island always on the list of excursions, and Paddington providing an excursion on most Sundays during the summer. Barry Island excursion traffic was a product of the steam age, and the change from steam to diesel and branch line closures coincided with a social change to car ownership and continental holidays, which quickly saw its demise.

Bank Holidays saw 5-minute intervals arrivals at Barry Island during the morning and early afternoon, most of the Rhondda, Rhymney and Sirhowy Valley excursions travelling over the former Barry Railway main line from Trehafod, Treforest or Penrhos Junction, with excursions from the Eastern and Western Valleys and GW/WR main line running via Dinas Powis. Trains returned from the Island again at 5-minute intervals from approx. 6-8pm, though in earlier days there were more late evening departures to give a longer day.

From the mid-nineteenth century, people had been travelling by horse-drawn coach from Cardiff and beyond to take the sea air for the day at Barry Island, which they reached by boat from the mainland, and which was then covered in waist-high grasses with few buildings. All this changed when the Barry Railway opened their Barry Island branch in 1896 and a Causeway road

was built alongside the Old Harbour. The opportunity was seized on by the Barry, Taff Vale and Rhymney Railway, LNWR and GWR to run to Barry through their running powers, though until the Grouping, the Barry ran empty trains into the Valleys to pick up this traffic, a feature that ceased in later years, the working pattern now based on incoming foreign power which normally spent the day on Barry shed, with main line engines (and initially empty trains with restaurant cars) returning to Canton for servicing, this being reduced only to large engines during the latter 1950s, with all servicing carried out in the High Level Sidings between Barry and Gladstone Bridge, the sidings being cleared of coal traffic for the purpose, which would have been impossible in earlier years.

Initially, there was resistance from some churchmen in the Valleys at the existence of Sunday excursions when parishioners should have been attending to their worship, but this was soon overcome with church and school parties, clubs, institutes and other groups chartering trains for their members to spend the day at the Island. The practice was mostly for the Barry Railway to run empty trains into the Valleys where they had running powers, pick up the passengers and run to the Island, the process being reversed in the evening, but some private companies ran their own excursions through to the Island. Probably the best known was the Abergavenny Brecon Road to Barry Island excursions run by the LNWR across the Merthyr Tredegar and Abergavenny (MT&A) line, examples of advertising brochures going back to 1905, the trains, of limited load, being initially worked by a pair of LNW Coal Tanks. These were so popular that they were full by the time they reached Brynmawr and an additional train had to be laid on from there. The same situation existed when the trains reached the Sirhowy line and an additional train was needed from Tredegar. Up to five trains were known to have run on this route on Summer Sundays.

Also under an arrangement with the Brecon & Merthyr (B&M) the Barry ran an empty train via Duffryn Isaf to Bassaleg where it and the crews remained overnight before continuing to Newport High Street on the Sunday morning and then running the excursion up the B&M back to Duffryn Isaf, with the B&M engine leading and the Barry as banker, before reversing at Duffryn Isaf and the Barry engine working the train back to Barry, the reverse arrangement pertaining for the return, though the Barry engine and crew returned immediately from Newport.

With the Grouping, a greater degree of through engine working began but the basic practice was still for the former Barry Company to work empty up the Valleys and return loaded. This was however an inefficient way to handle the traffic and the Valley depots began to work the trains from their home stations through to the Island, remaining at Barry until the evening return. To do so however required room for stabling the empty stock, though some returned for a second run. In 1929, Barry Island station was remodelled to provide additional platforms and stabling sidings, including using Barry Pier station. With the reduction in shipment coal during the 1930s, it was also possible to make room at the High Level Sidings, between Barry Engine Works and west of Barry Dock Station, to stable excursion stock on Sundays, by filling the tip roads with coal wagons and fully using accommodation elsewhere. This enabled the excursion stock to be taken from the Island and held until their return working, a practice that pertained until the demise of the traffic in the late 1960s. The engines were serviced on Barry Shed and the crews enjoyed a day at the Island.

The local Barry photographer Gerard Hubback took a series of excellent photographs in the mid-1930s of excursions to Barry Island and the following are my selection of the best. They are undated but are probably from 1935-38.

En route to Barry Island Old Oak Common Castle 5045, whose name was changed from *Bridgwater Castle* to *Earl of Dudley* in September 1937, heads a Holiday Haunts Express past the Merch Bridge at Dinas Powis. As the negative has no date, it is not possible to give the exact engine name.

There seems to have been a regular Sunday excursion from Paddington to Barry Island in the 1930s, and here Old Oak's 4009 *Shooting Star*, rebuilt from a Star in 1925, and renamed 100 *A1 Lloyds* in January 1936, runs between Barry Dock and Barry probably in 1935.

Old Oak Common's Hall 5936 *Oakley Hall*, new in July 1933, heads an excursion to the Island with a clerestory brake third leading, as the train passes Gladstone Bridge, near the Western Welsh garage.

Another historical Castle; London based, the converted Great Bear No. 111 passes Barry Syndicate Sidings with what may well be a Swindon Works Holiday excursion with such a reporting number as 39, the engine now named *Viscount Churchill* since rebuilding as a Castle.

Stars were also regular visitors in the 1930s, and here 4018 *Knight of the Grand Cross* runs along the Causeway with an excursion from Worcester, the train headed by a clerestory brake third.

Taunton Star 4054 *Princess Alexandra* runs alongside the High Level Sidings between Barry Dock and Barry stations with the Sunday excursion from Paddington 010. 4054 was based at Taunton throughout the late 1930s and was presumably borrowed by Old Oak for a day trip to Barry.

The epitome of Barry in the 1930s as Old Oak Castle 5052 *Earl of Radnor* passes wagons of shipment coal on both sides at Cadoxton with the evening return train. This is dated to either late summer 1937 or summer 1938 by the fact the engine was renamed to an Earl in July 1937 and is definitely carrying an Earl name in the picture. Again, the standard clerestory brake third is conveyed front.

The Sunday Paddington to Barry Island excursion, carrying reporting number 180, ariving at Barry behind Old Oak Castle 4084 *Aberystwyth Castle*. ... and the return train leaving Barry Island with an articulated set on the front of the train.

5055 Earl of Eldon is in charge of the Paddington to Barry island excursion as it passes the High Level Sidings where stock off other excursions is berthed in this late 1930s scene.

The now preserved 4965 Rood Aston Hall rounds the bend off the Barry Island branch with a return excursion, once again with a clerestory brake third on the front.

Converted Star 4037 Queen Philippa runs along the Causeway into Barry Island with another excursion from Paddington carrying reporting number 180. This engine was renamed The South Wales Borderers in March 1937, but is definitely carrying the Queen nameplate here, dating the photograph to probably summer 1936.

Finally in this 1930s cameo, an excursion from Barry to London conveying members of the Barry Conservative Association, two trains of empty stock standing at Ship Hill Bridge in 1933 awaiting entry into Barry station, with Canton's 4099 Kilgerran Castle on the nearest train, both having a clerestory brake third leading.

A view of the station from Barry Island West SB steps on 27 August 1961 with 7310 on a return Wrexham excursion at Platform 1 with the Loco. Inspector chatting to the crew.

The Great Western were very much into excursion traffic, especially on Summer and bank holiday weekends, and Barry Island was the top seaside resort for such trains in South Wales. Regular excursions were run on Sundays from Paddington, with paths in the Working Timetables, arrivals being at lunch time with return at 6.35 or 6.55pm, worked from the 1920s to the 1960s by Old Oak Common Stars and Castles, plus just one example of a Britannia (70023 which was the first of the Class to visit Barry).

Excursions ran from many other main line locations, hauled through to Barry Island by 4-6-0s or 2-6-0s. The latter could be turned at Barry via the Dock lines and then remained on Barry shed until their return working, but anything larger had to be sent to Canton for turning and servicing. One occasion during the mid-1930s deserves special mention when no fewer than ten excursions were run from Dudley, as that population took over the Island for the day.

The classic shot of a Paddington return excursion leaving Barry Island and passing the West box on 6 August 1961, behind Old Oak Common's 5082 Swordfish. The engine will have returned to Canton for servicing but the stock was stabled in the High Level Sidings.

Lesser power is provided for this Cheltenham excursion with Gloucester's 6365 in charge in August 1961. The engine will have been turned on the dock lines, enabling the crew to enjoy the day at Barry.

A feature of the 1956/7 seasons was the re-introduction of the Holiday Express with engines carrying a large round headboard on the front. Here 7912 Little Linford Hall comes off the Barry island branch with the City of Birmingham Holiday Express on 6 August 1956.

Here 5004 Llanstephan Castle rounds the bend at the end of the Barry Island branch with the Shropshire Holiday Express on 6 August 1957.

5040 Stokesay Castle approaches Barry Dock station with a Sunday excursion from Paddington on 19 May 1957.

Hall 5965 Woollas Hall heads past Barry Dock station with a return excursion.

Rounding the bend at Barry Dock, 5331 of Oxley shed heads an excursion from Birmingham on 6 April 1953.

Gloucester's 6373 approaches Barry station with an excursion from Cheltenham on 19 May 1957, formed of headboarded Mark 1 stock off a Cheltenham-London service.

Gloucester's 6317 rounds the bend onto the Barry Island branch in 1958, passing Barry Junction SB which was burnt out and never re-opened, with an excursion from Gloucester.

A view taken from the bedroom window of our house in Dock View Road showing Old Oak Common's 7001 Sir James Milne between Cadoxton and Barry Dock stations with an excursion from Paddington, with Barry Docks Storage Sidings in the background.

Barry Island East with 6856 Stowe Grange of Worcester shed with the empty stock of a return Evesham charter special awaiting entry into the platform on 18 August 1963, with a DMU standing in Platform 2.
S. Rickard/J&J Collection.

Standing in the spur at Barry Island West, Castle 5082 Swordfish awaits the arrival of its empty stock from the High Level Sidings for return to Paddington on 6 August 1961.

Two Halls, with Modified 7918 Rhose Wood Hall off an excursion from Birmingham leading, head off to Canton for servicing past the Barry Island starter somersault signal on 24 May 1953.

Barry Island station on August Bank Holiday Sunday 6 August 1961 with a 56XX on a return Valleys train at Platform 1, a 94XX running bunker first on a return Newport excursion at Platform 3 and County 1025 County of Radnor on a return Tyseley excursion at Platform 4.

5625 pulls out of Platform 4 at Barry Island with a return Blaenavon excursion on 27 August 1961 with crowds waiting on Platform 1. The bus and car park behind was one of the main parking areas for Western Welsh and other buses that had brought parties to the seaside for the day.

6663 with a return Western Valley excursion to Brynmawr passing Cadoxton Low Level on 26 May 1961.

6663 again with a return excursion to the Western Valley passing Cadoxton Low Level with the reporting number carried on the top lamp bracket by its Aberbeeg crew. The coal hoists of No. 2 Dock can be seen in the background.

A summer 1961 scene at Barry Island with strong evening sun, with a 56XX at Platform 1 with a return Valleys excursion, 2218 at Platform 3 bound for Newport and a main line excursion at Platform 4 with a Grange 4-6-0.

5661 departs from Platform 3 at Barry Island with 2Z01 a return excursion to Merthyr in 1961.

Newport excursions were often worked by one of Ebbw Junction's 2251 Class, as here with 2218 rounding the bend onto the Barry Island branch on 12 May 1957.

Double heading on excursions was a rarity but here Ebbw's 3170 and 5173 are in the yard at Barry Island to work a return excursion to Chepstow on 21 June 1968.

And here two Radyr 56xxs, led by 6684 battle with a gale force wind as they pass Cadoxton North with a return excustion to Treherbert formed with main line stock on 14 June 1959.

5692 of Radyr runs along the south face of the island platform at Barry with an extended Queen Street to Barry Island special in May 1958.

Barry's 6614 has had to replace the Pontypool Road engine that should have worked this return excursion to Pontypool and is seen with its ten coach train east of Cadoxton, with wagons of shipment coal in the sidings alongside.

Ebbw's Mogul 7319 about to cross the junction with the Vale of Glamrogan line at Barry with a return excursion to Newport.

A contrast in motive power for this weekday return Newport excursion, the empty stock for which is being worked from the High Level Sidings through Barry station to Barry Island by Ebbw's 7775 on 6 August 1957.

The opposite contrast in motive power in the form of a Grange 6823 Oakley Grange approaching Barry Dock station with an excursion also from Newport on 10 June 1957.

The star turn on the local excursions was undoubtedly the regular excursion from Nantybwch, hauled by a Tredegar LNW 0-8-0. Here 49064 on the down train approaches Barry Dock station on 10 June 1957.

A rare chance to see an LNW 0-8-0 carrying a WR Reporting Number, as 49064 heads past Cadoxton Low Level with the 7.35pm return excursion to Nantybwch on 26 May 1958.

The down Nantybwch excursion leaves Barry for the Island and is also seen running into Barry with 49064 in charge, in both cases carrying the usual number 56.

An unusual view of the 0-8-0 working the empty stock of its down train back through Barry to be stored in the High Level Sidings for the day in May 1958, with 49409 in charge.

The return Nanybwch excursion takes the former Barry Railway route through Wenvoe past the huge shipment coal yard at Cadoxton behind 49121 on 25 May 1958.

The No. 11 excursion from Senghenydd leaves the Penarth branch at Biglis Junction behind a Cathays 56XX in summer 1958. The first coach is a former LMS vehicle which came from the MT&A line when that closed to passengers in January 1958.

August Bank Holiday 1963 and Class 37 diesels had replaced steam on much of the Valleys working as here with a return excursion to Bargoed departing from Platform 4 at Barry Island.

From 1958, the introduction of DMUs started to impact on the Island working, but a six coach DMU could only provide 524 seats and when heavy overcrowding took place (as it regularly did) problems with closing the doors occurred due to the stress on the solebars. Steam stock thus continued to be necessary to handle the passenger volumes and trains of up to ten coaches ran regularly from the Eastern and Western Valleys until their demise in 1962, suitably banked from Newport on their return. The closure of several Valley lines impacted heavily on excursion traffic until by 1963 it was possible to run the whole of the remaining service with DMUs. There was little involvement of the Type 3 diesel engines on excursions to the island, just a few examples being recorded. Similarly, some examples of diesels occurred on main line excursions in the mid-1960s, but by then the traffic was suffering badly from car and coach traffic and also from continental holidays, which proved the death knell for what had been a most thriving and lucrative traffic for over fifty years, though one costly in terms of the amount of spare stock it involved.

Photographs of the now preserved and renamed Hall 4965 Rood Aston Hall are apparently hard to find, but here is another of the engine passing Palmerston with the 7.40pm return excursion from Barry Island to Tyseley on 25th May 1958, with wagons of shipment coal in the sidings alongside.

CHAPTER 10

MAIN LINE DIVERSIONS

A HIGHLIGHT ON several Sundays during the Winter service from September to May and one which still continues, was the diversion of trains from the main line between Cardiff and Bridgend to run via Barry and the Vale of Glamorgan from midnight on Sunday morning until varying times on the Sunday night/Monday morning, dependent on the time required to complete the work. This practice was organised between the Civil Engineer at Newport and the Operating Superintendent at Cardiff and was a regular feature most years. The largely two track railway on the main line between Cardiff and Bridgend would be handed over completely to the Engineer for him to replace track, renew bridges or carry out other work at one or more locations. Cranes could stand on one line while the other was being renewed and the engineering operation greatly facilitated. District Inspectors and SM/AM Barry were in charge of the working from start to completion in case any problems were encountered which required the intervention of the Operating department. All signal boxes along the diversionary route were opened.

Barry depot supplied pilot drivers when main line men did not know the road, but it was normal for Canton and Landore men who worked the majority of the trains not to require them. It was only when a special freight perhaps worked by Severn Tunnel, Ebbw or Neath men was diverted that a pilotman was required, though there were very few Sunday freights in steam days. This situation has changed in the modern era with the number of inter-steelworks trains running on Sundays to and from Port Talbot

Works.

Restricted working was involved when coaching stock of 70ft. in length was formed into trains and trains were not allowed to pass each other at Barry Dock station, the practice being for up trains to be held at the up starting signal at the east end of the station platform. Just why this restriction existed always baffled me as Barry Dock station was an island platform, so any possible confliction must have concerned the point at which the up and down tracks came together again east of the station, but this was only a surmise. I could never understand how, if such trains could pass on the tight curve through Cogan station, they could not pass at Barry Dock.

The first up train on a Sunday morning was the 6.45am Fishguard Harbour to Paddington, the punctuality of which was very much down to the weather. I was normally out with my camera to record this and later services and several excellent shots accompany this section. Services were steam hauled until 1962 when Hymek diesels first appeared on the London services. By the next year these were hauled by Western Class diesel hydraulics and Brush Type 4s and these held sway until the introduction of the Class 253 High Speed Units in 1976.

In addition to planned weekend engineering work, ad hoc diversions sometimes took place on weekdays due to one-off incidents such as points or signal failures etc. These were arranged as they occurred through the Control and lasted only as long as the incident. The normal Valleys passenger and freight service had to continue to run, albeit with delay, as the main line diverted trains had priority.

Canton's 5010 Restormel Castle approaches Porthkerry Viaduct with the diverted 9.55am Paddington to Swansea service in the late 1940s

The late 1940s when Counties were at work on London services as 1012 County of Denbigh runs through Porthkerry Park with an up service to Paddington.

Canton's 5030 Shirburn Castle runs through Barry station with the 9.5am Bristol to Swansea on 4 May 1958.

The now preserved 5051 Earl Bathurst of Landore heads the 6.45am Fishguard Harbour to Paddington passing under Ship Hill Bridge on 4 May 1958.

Old Oak Common's 5014 Goodrich Castle with the 10.55am Swansea to Sheffield which it will work to Banbury approaching Ship Hill Bridge at Barry on 27 April 1958.

The 9.55am Paddington to Swansea runs past the High Level Sidings which were cleared of coal wagons on summer weekends for storage of excursion empty stock. This view on 27 April 1958.

Canton Britannia 70025 Western Star passes under Ship Hill Bridge with the 9.15am Bristol to Swansea on 27 April 1958. Later it will return with the 4.10pm Whitland to Kensington Milk, working as far as Cardiff.

There was not normally much freight in evidence on diversion days but here 3847 runs down the relief line between Barry Junction and Barry Sidings with a military special bringing back tanks from Suez for Pembrokeshire.

5091 Cleeve Abbey between Barry and Barry Dock passing the Western Welsh garage with the 6.45am Fishguard Harbour to Paddington.

Barry Sidings Yard is seen on the left at Canton Britannia 70025 Western Star runs along the original Vale of Glamorgan Railway line out of Barry with the 9.15am Bristol to Swansea on 27 April 1958.

Excursion Traffic • **161**

Sunday 25 September 1960 offered lovely sunny conditions for the camera as evidenced here with 4093 Dunster Castle heading through Barry Station with the 6.45am Fishguard Harbour to Paddington, soon followed on the down by 5909 Newton Hall running with just a single passenger brakevan and no empty milk tanks on the 4.10am Marston to Whitland, photographed from Barry Signalbox window.

There were then two freights, first the 7.30am Margam to Severn Tunnel whose 6620 stopped at Barry to take water and then a 10.30am Pontypool Ropad to Margam whose train engine 5248 was assisted up Porthkerry bank from Barry Sidings by 5619, its load headed by cattle wagons being returned for cleaning at Carmarthen for supply to Fishguard Harbour probably for imported Irish cattle to Smithfield traffic. This traffic ceased to be carried by rail in 1962.

70018 Flying Dutchman worked the 9.55am Paddington to Swansea, here seen between Ship Hill Bridge and Barry Sidings while a gleaming 7037 Swindon had the 11.20am Carmarthen to Paddington seen passing Barry Sidings SB.

A March 1962 diversion was probably the last in steam days before the Hymeks took over and here 5078 Beaufort passes through Palmerston, east of Cadoxton with the 6.45am Fishguard Harbour to Paddington.

The change from steam to diesel was made progressively during 1962 and Hymek 1700HP diesels were introduced into the South Wales to London and Shrewsbury turns. On a diversion in late 1962, Hymek D7026 runs through Barry with the 6.45am Fishguard Harbour to Paddington, in a view taken from the signal box.

The same train passing Gladstone Bridge between Barry and Barry Dock on a misty Sunday morning with a Hymek in charge.

Another Hymek on the 9.55am Paddington to Swansea passing under Ship Hill bridge in late 1962.

Western Class Diesel D10XX rounds the curve through Barry Dock station with the 11.20am Carmarthen to Paddington in Winter 1963.

A nice study of a Western Class Diesel leaving Porthkerry Tunnel with the 11.20am Carmarthen to Paddington in 1963.

D1012 Western Firebrand passes through Barry station with the 6.45am Fishguard Harbour to Paddington on 25 May 1963.

A Brush 2700HP Diesel passes Cadoxton with the 10am Paddington to Swansea in 1964.

D1000 Western Enterprise runs between Barry Dock and Cadoxton beneath the substantial rock cliff with a Carmarthen to Paddington service in the first diversion of the Winter service 1963-4.

D1008 Western Harrier in the same position as the picture of Castle 111 Viscount Churchill earlier in the book (*p131*), rounding the bend through Barry Dock, in the 1963-4 diversions with a Paddington to Swansea train.

Running between Barry Dock and Cadoxton stations, D1061 Western Envoy with a Swansea to Paddington service in 1963-4.

D1014 Western Leviathan on a weekday diversion passing Barry with the 3pm Paddington to Swansea on 5 April 1964.

Inter City three-car set passing Barry box with the 9.30am Bristol to Swansea, now running as a DMU vice engine and coaches on 25 September 1960.

An original Inter City set on a Birmingham to Swansea service passing Barry Sidings on 28 September 1957.

In the early diesel age when the lines to the Docks from Cadoxton Low Level into the Tunnel were in the process of being reduced to just serve the New (No. 2) Dock. The lines previously serving No. 1 Dock have been retained and have been slewed to become the new lines into No. 2 Dock. D6844 is passing on the main line with an up short engineer's train in a mid-1960s picture. Our family house can be seen third along from the Sea View Labour Club in the centre of the picture.

Weekday diversions were a rarity and always happened at very short notice as here in an evening in 1958 when the Up South Wales Pullman was recorded passing Barry station with 5041 Tiverton Castle and the down 2.55pm Paddington to Swansea with the now preserved 5043 Earl of Mount Edgecumbe.

CHAPTER 11

WOODHAM'S SCRAPYARD

THE WOODHAM FAMILY had run a business at Barry Dock since the time it was opened in 1889, functioning as a family business, with their company Woodham & Sons established in 1892. This would have been by Dai Woodham's grandfather who made a business out of recovering redundant ropes and tackle, scrap metal and packing of various types used to separate and protect cargoes in transit across the seas and disposing of them if now useless or selling them on for other use. He also ran a general porterage business on the dock, moving materials and equipment to wherever it was necessary, working from their yard in Thomson Street. The firm was involved in the arrangements for the opening ceremony of the dock in July 1889. Such a type of business can go unnoticed for many years until some event catches the public eye and lifts the business from the unknown to put it in the public eye. It would be over fifty years before such an event took place in the history of the business, by which time ownership had passed to David Lloyd Victor Woodham, known as Dai, born in 1919, whose father Albert had retired from the business in 1947. Dai, then 28, took over the business, and in 1953 re-organised it into four separate companies – Woodham Brothers, Woodham Transport, Woodham Marine and Woodham metals. Between the four concerns, they employed 200 staff, largely on the docks.

The British Railways Modernisation Plan of 1955 sought to make inroads into the old out-of-date equipment and to introduce new. It was in the scrapping of the older unfitted (non-vacuum-brake-fitted) freight wagons that was the opportunity for the outside scrap merchants to join the 'gravy train' (as Dai called it). This was Woodham's introduction into the changing railway scene, and long rakes of condemned unfitted vans would appear at and gradually disappear from the railway sidings to be scrapped on the dock in what was an easy procedure of burning the wooden bodies and cutting through the underframes to expose the wheels and axles which could be supplied to the steelworks at home or exported abroad. Unfitted vans soon became a thing of the past as modern (though same size) vacuum-fitted vans were turned out from the builders.

The wagon fleet was to be reduced from 1.25 million vehicles to 600,000, so those involved enjoyed years of prosperity that the railway regions really wanted no part of as they had better things to do than to break up wagons. By the mid-1950s, Woodham Bros. had transferred most of their activity into the scrap metal market and were producing high quality scrap metal for the newly nationalised steel industry in South Wales, drawn largely from redundant track and wagons. Condemned wagons needed to be stored away from the operating railway and an agreement was entered into between Woodhams and the British Transport Docks Board to take over sidings on the recently filled West Pond site, alongside Barry Engine Works and at Barry Island for the storage of condemned stock.

1958 saw the introduction of Diesel Multiple Units on the Cardiff Valleys Passenger service, rendering redundant the older passenger stock which again found its way after auction into Woodham's clutches. Rows of redundant Valleys passenger coaches, added to when Beeching closed several lines in the area, used to appear in front of our house in the Storage Sidings, being then taken away for burning out and cutting up.

But it was the region-wide introduction of diesel shunting engines and main line diesels in the West of England that created a surplus of steam engine stock starting in 1959 that really started the ball rolling for Dai Woodham. A decision was made by Western Region management that with the large number of engines that would now be withdrawn from service in the plan to make the region the first to be completely dieselised, this was beyond the capability of the Works to handle, and that the redundant engines should be sold to scrap merchants. Scrapping engines was a more complicated procedure than scrapping wagons or coaches as there were valuable metals involved which needed expert handling and disposal. Dealings were opened up with those scrap merchants who gave notice that they wished to be involved in the scrapping business. Dai Woodham went to Swindon for a week's course in how to scrap steam engines, no doubt with the promise of much business in the future. Scrapping of engines at Swindon Works was carried out at C Shop where he probably spent much of his time there on practical demonstration. It was not long before the wheels of the new scrapping business were set in motion.

There were two batches of engines sent from Swindon Works in March 1959 to South Wales breakers. First, a group of four 14XX 0-4-2Ts, which had been previously engaged on auto working, were sent to breakers in the upper Rhymney Valley, and on 25 March, four mixed traffic 2-6-0s, now replaced by more modern 4-6-0s, Nos. 5312/60/92/97 were sent to Woodhams,

with an additional single engine No. 3170 a week later. Four more of the 2-6-0s arrived in the August. Dai Woodham's gravy train had started to arrive.

Other smaller concerns also sprang up in the Barry area eager to get in on the act of breaking up redundant engines. One such concern was J.O. Williams who took engines and wagons into their area on the Dock for breaking up. By 1963, a contract had been let to R.S. Tyley Ltd., for the recovery and disposal of all the track from Cadoxton Yard at Palmerston, all thirty-seven tracks and adjuncts, as the start of recovering the whole of the closed branch line to Treforest and Trehafod. Also, Woodfields began operations at the now closed Cadoxton Station Yard, from where domestic coal traffic had been moved to the new Coal Concentration at Barry Goods at the west end of No.1 Dock. Barry had been transformed into a veritable town of scrap, with much being exported through the Dock.

Condemned engines continued to arrive either formed into freight services or running as short specials and following the introduction of Hymek diesels onto the London and Shrewsbury services in 1962, two Kings (Nos 6023/4), though barred from the Barry route, found themselves sold to Woodham after being refused permission to be hauled to T.W. Ward at Briton Ferry. By the end of 1965, condemned engines delivered to Woodham amounted to about 150 and were held both on the West Pond site and around the former Barry Works and Barry Goods. But rakes of wagons were also arriving for which accommodation needed to be found. Wagons could be disposed of far more quickly and easily than engines and so Dai Woodham ceased the slow process of cutting up engines to concentrate on wagons and brakevans, in order that room could be found to receive more and more of the latter into the operating sidings, while the engines languished in the West Pond site and other areas now rented by him from the Docks Board. January 1968 saw over 200 engines from the Western, Southern and London Midland Regions, a fantastic array, which attracted attention from enthusiasts all over the country, when later in that year, a development occurred which changed the whole of the engine scene. The Keighley & Worth Valley Railway approached Woodham to purchase a Fowler 4F 0-6-0 No. 43924. Their purchase was successful and in September the engine was taken away on a low-loader for the long journey north.

This was to be a turning point in the whole story of the Woodham scrapyard as this purchase triggered action by preservation societies to purchase engines from them, where the engines soon became plastered with notices of ownership or intended ownership and Woodham became content to concentrate his business on the continuing flow of condemned wagons and to see what the future held for the engines, many of which were now earmarked by preservationists. By the end of 1970, eleven engines had been purchased for preservation, but this still left over 200 on site. Though some scrapping did continue, for example of diesel engines which the preservationists seemed to have no interest in, despite the stock containing the former WR main line diesels D600 and D601, the decision seemed to have been to leave the steam engines alone for the developing business of purchasing for the heritage railways. The mid-1970s saw sixty-one engines rescued from the scrapyard between 1972-75, with great interest still being expressed in many of the remaining engines, some by now rusting wrecks as the salt air ate into the metal. Between 1976 and 1980 a further thirty-nine engines were purchased and in 1981 alone a further twenty. Such was the level of interest and concern that the stock of engines, the only such stock

left in the country, should be conserved, that societies for their conservation were formed with even questions in the House.

Following Dai Woodham's retirement, various concerns became involved in ensuring that the remaining engines were properly protected. Eventually the number left dwindled to ten and it was felt that these should now be protected from the elements as they were of considerable sentimental and historical value. They were therefore taken from the docks site to be housed in the now empty former Western Welsh garage in Broad Street. By now the preservation movement, which was now a thriving concern, was including building new examples of classes which had disappeared over the years, and it was found that the Barry Ten contained examples of boilers and other parts that could be used in the re-creation of several of the new builds, such as the Saint and County Classes, and the rusting hulks became the source for spare and replacement parts and this continues to this day.

The preservation movement in this country owes a huge debt of gratitude to Dai Woodham and his decision to stop cutting up his fleet of condemned engines and to concentrate on wagons, coaches and brakevans. The two Kings now running at Didcot, the two Somerset & Dorset 2-8-0s, and the Jubilees are a few examples of the prizes of which, without Dai Woodham, we would be deprived. Unfortunately, a few examples slipped through which would have been prizes for retention, such as No. 3170, the last of the 3150 Class, the fifth engine to arrive at Woodhams, but we must forgive this 1959 phenomenon. Had Dai lived on beyond his 75th year, perhaps he would have been honoured for his service to the preservation of steam engines in the country. He certainly deserved to be. Dai Woodham 1919-94 RIP.

An overall view of the Woodham West Pond site as seen from the approach to Barry Island. M.B.Warburton

In the early 1960s, it was almost all Western Region engines which arrived as seen here with two 42XXs and two 4575s with 6023/4 behind. Other 45s are seen in the distance.

A close-up of the two Kings 6024 (double chimney – front) and 6023 (single chimney – rear) which both arrived together from Canton. 6024 would go on to be restored at Didcot and have many fine exploits on the main line while 6023 would be restored later and kept as a single chimney example. Mike Back Colln.

A pair of condemned rebuilt Merchant Navies head a line of Halls and other SR Pacifics, the front engines being 35025 and 35009.

The WR 4500 and 4575 Class faced early withdrawal as their branch line operations had either been converted to diesel multiple unit or else closed. Here a rake of these engines stands behind a SR streamlined Pacific in 1968. Mike Back Colln.

Manors were always high on the preservationists interest when Woodhams entered that phase in the 1970s. A light 4-6-0, originally converted from 43XX 2-6-0s, they were ideal for being powerful with a high route availability. Here 7827 sits in the yard, soon to be taken away for restoration. Mike Back Colln.

Several of the Standard Class 4 2-6-4Ts appeared, and 80151 was taken off by the Bluebell Railway and is now a regular performer on their line between Sheffield Park and East Grinstead. I always wish these engines had been tried in the South Wales Valleys instead of the Standard Class 3 2-6-2Ts which proved underpowered but the WR never used the class until 1963 largely in the Swansea area. Mike Back Colln.

A streamlined light Pacific stands at the head of a row of panniers and other classes with at least three other rows visible. Mike Back Colln.

Woodham also rented sidings alongside the former Barry Engine Works and here we see former SR 2-6-0 31674 parked next to a Hall.

Two Battle of Britain light Pacifics stand together, 34092 and 34072.

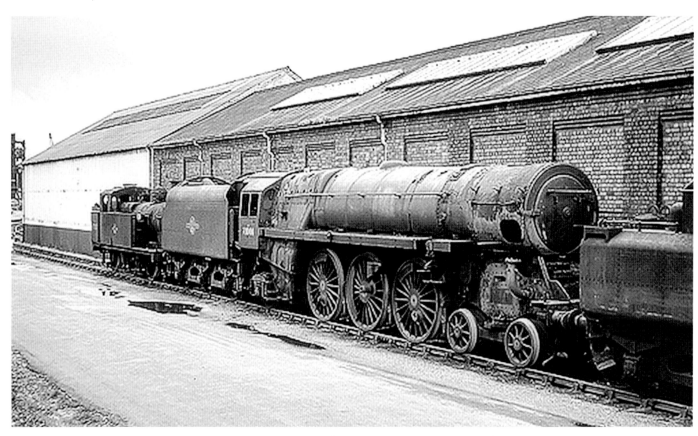

After being received into Barry Dock Storage Sidings, 71000 (the former Duke of Gloucester) was moved to stand alongside the former Barry Goods at the west end of No.1 Dock, from where it was moved to stand on the West Pond site. These two views show it in both positions.

Here we see three SR 4-6-0s as they arrived at Barry Dock Storage Sidings with barrier wagons between. The leading two are 30499 and 30841.

Standing in the High Level Sidings alongside Barry Engine Works, SR U Class 31618, now restored on the Bluebell Railway stands next to 53808.

Early arrivals were these 0-6-0 tanks from the Longmoor Military Railway, but they appear to have been all cut up.

One of the most interesting engines to be held was this former Somerset and Dorset 7F 2-8-0 53808 which is now back restored and running well though not on its previous route between Bath and Bournemouth which did not survive the Beeching cuts.

Instead of cutting up locomotives, Woodham scrapped rolling stock. This interesting collection of wooden hoppers received from the north-east was photographed in Barry Dock Storage Sidings.

Another type received in quantity were brakevans such as this selection again photographed in Barry Dock Storage Sidings.

CHAPTER 12

THE PRESENT SCENE

DURING THE 1970S, the railway scene at Barry had dwindled to a low ebb. The valley passenger business was suffering badly from the onslaught of the private car and several of the branch lines feeding into the main Valley north to south routes had closed. This had led the local Divisional management to seek economies by reducing the main service level and it was not uncommon during the evening to have to wait an hour between trains on the Barry line, an approach which is usually counter-productive. The gloom was however often punctuated by the removal of another of the Woodham engines by low-loader off to enjoy a resurrected life on a heritage railway in some part of the country.

Coal traffic through the Docks had finished, Geest banana traffic had moved to Southampton, the engine works had closed, the excursion traffic had dried up by rail, with the line across the Causeway from Barry to Barry Island singled in 1969 and the two branches to Bridgend and Pontypridd both closed. On the freight side, there was still some business to be had from the high capacity cranes at the east end of the New Dock, with bulk cargoes such as imported coal, phosphate rock, and manganese ore, but these had an uncertain future in competition with Newport and Avonmouth. The only large-scale traffic with a long-term future was the coal traffic to Aberthaw B Power Station. The A station had not developed beyond its early capacity but the B station was now taking coal by Merry Go Round 32ton wagon trains from a variety of collieries and opencast in the Valleys. There was still some traffic to and from Aberthaw Cement Works and Dow

Corning via the No. 2 Dock lines. The number of scrapped engines remaining in Woodham's sidings at the west end of No. 1 Dock was going down as preservation societies scraped up enough cash to purchase yet another. Finally, the Vale of Glamorgan Council arranged to house the remaining ten in the now empty local Western Welsh bus garage. A preservation society was being developed at Barry Island using now redundant facilities.

The regeneration of the Valley services which began in the 1980s under the direction of the Manager, Wales, my friend John Davies, breathed new life into travel between Barry and Cardiff. This was based on a frequent interval service, using two-car trains with ticket sales and inspection on train, though booking offices were open in the morning peak. With three main starting points in the valleys, there could now be a 20-minute interval service through to Barry Island throughout the day, a vast improvement on some of the hour waits on a bleak Platform 7 at Cardiff General in the 1970s for an evening train to Barry. With the Aberdare and Maesteg services restored, capitalising on the fact that the double track main line between Barry and Bridgend was still in use for coal trains to Aberthaw Power Station, Ford Motor Company trains to Bridgend and as a main line diversionary route, a case for reopening the passenger service between Barry and Bridgend, with a bus link from Rhoose to Cardiff Airport, was supported and implemented from 2005. The new service is extremely well used in the peak hours and the 0742 Bridgend to Aberdare is full leaving Rhoose at 0806, so passengers joining at Barry and beyond have to stand. Return evening peak services from Cardiff Central at 1641 and 1741 are equally well used. A case has been discussed for providing a half hourly interval, at least during the peak. The majority of the traffic is Cardiff commuter which is in keeping with much of the traffic across the Cardiff Valleys. Similarly, the line to Ebbw Vale has been re-opened and already has had to be doubled between Risca and Llanhilleth due to plans to double the frequency of services. Congested roads in the Cardiff and Newport Valleys have caused the regeneration of rail services. This situation applies also on the roads between Cardiff and Barry, the 'top' road via Wenvoe and the 'lower' road via Dinas Powis with large queues through this popular residential area.

On the freight side, the main traffic on the Barry line is coal to Aberthaw B Power Station. In some years re-stocking has lifted the service to some ten trains a day, but currently this is reduced to about three, the main supply point being Cwmbargoed from Ffos y Fran, though previously a significant amount was imported through Avonmouth. Traffic was first conveyed in 32ton MGR wagons but these days it is all in 100ton hoppers, many of which unfortunately carry a lot of graffiti on their sides. With the likelihood that coal fired stations are to be phased out, the future of this traffic must be considered uncertain.

Chemical traffic to and from Dow Corning at Cadoxton, served via the No. 2 Dock lines, continues in 100ton tanks and other wagons and as far as is known this is long term. New flows of traffic have recently been developed from Tarmac's Aberthaw Cement Works in tankers to Moorswater and Westbury with loaded outwards and return empties and Class 70 locos.

In 1995 a Class 56 runs along the north side of No. 2 Dock with the evening chemicals train from Dow Corning Chemical Plant to Blackpool.

In 1995 the evening chemicals train to Blackpool is seen rounding the bend at the west end of No. 2 Dock heading for Graving Dock Junction with 56044 piloting another Class 56 en route to Crewe Works.

The big question posing itself throughout the valley lines is however what will happen under electrification and under the mooted Metro system for South Wales whereby a light rail (Tram) system would connect into the conventional rail system at nominated points? This would hopefully go some way to restoring an improved transport system to locations which were deprived of their local rail service during the 1960s, and might hopefully include linking the Sirhowy Valley into either the Rhymney Valley or into an improved Western Valley service, linking the Rhondda Fach into through services at Porth, and closed stations above Maesteg into the re-instated Maesteg service. Within this should be considered the possibility of extending the 'heavy' rail system into such areas. One of the benefits of the development of a light rail system would be to avoid the slowness and delays of bus transport on heavily congested roads in South Wales.

It is however the overall effect of

electrification which would appear the most significant development as far as the future of Barry is concerned. This has now been replanned to operate only as far as Cardiff, power cars being fitted with diesel engines to cover unelectrified sections. This will mean that the line from Cardiff to Bridgend via Barry (the present diversionary route) will not be electrified under the main line scheme, but will (hopefully) under the Valleys scheme. This is being strongly resisted and my summary is correct only at the time of writing.

The Valley lines north of Cardiff have no appreciable infrastructure to raise the cost of electrification, so it seems probable that these would also be equipped with overhead wires, once the payment of the associated cost can be agreed. This would hopefully enable line speeds to be raised by redesigning curves to provide canting and raising the speed through many of the junctions which are a significant drag on journey times at present, many speed restrictions on the line having been set for close-coupled steam engines. The lines around Cardiff Central have many such heavy speed restrictions which should not apply to unit traffic and which could

bring down the overall journey time from Cardiff to Barry appreciably. The future should be intriguing if the right priorities are adopted and the necessary monies made available. The diesel units used on the Valley lines are old and slow as are the line speeds. The post electrification journey time from Barry to Cardiff should be no longer than 15mins.

The passenger service seems set to become part of the South Wales Metro, though, from what I can see, unchanged from what it is currently as far as Barry is concerned. There must be a big question mark hanging over the future of Aberthaw B coal-fired power station in view of the intention to eliminate such installations, though it seems a case of 'if and when'. The biggest question seems to be around the long term future of the docks. Though the north side of No. 1 is now the Waterfront development, will the dock itself remain, little progress having been made to attract water craft? Will it ultimately be filled in and the area redeveloped? And what of No. 2 Dock, still operational but standing completely empty most of the time? Perhaps there are still interesting times ahead, let us hope so.

A Class 47 leaves Porthkerry Tunnel with the down Mail service on 7 July 1998. M.J. Back.

The Mail service runs across Porthkerry Viaduct with a Class 47 in charge on 29t June 1998. M.J. Back

An up oil service with 100ton tankers runs through Barry station behind a Class 37 in 1993.

Class 60 60068 runs through No. 2 Porthkerry Tunnel with a train of empty MGR wagons for Tower Colliery on 10 July 1998 and crosses the Viaduct. Both M.J. Back.

A vantage point no more. A Class 37 runs onto the down loop at Barry SB with a train of empty MGR wagons for maintenance at Barry in 1995.

Type 3 37704 runs past Barry box with another load of coal for Aberthaw from the Valleys.

An up train of empty MGR wagons from Aberthaw B passes through Barry behind Class 66 66184 in May 2001.

A down loaded MGR train passes through Barry seen from the passenger footbridge.

Approaching Gladstone Bridge, 66004 heads east with a train of MGR wagons from Aberthaw on 21 May 2001.

Crossing the junction with the Barry Island branch at the west end of the station, 66092 heads a train of empty 100tonners back from Aberthaw.

Another view taken from the new Gladstone Bridge 66199 is between Barry Docks and Barry stations with a morning Avonmouth to Aberthaw train on 21 May 2001.

100 ton wagons have now replaced the 32 ton MGR wagons on the Aberthaw working, and here a 66XXX emerges from Porthkerry tunnel with an up afternoon service in 2007.

In a view from the former Barry signalbox in September 2007, a down train of 100tonners heads for Aberthaw with a 66XXX in charge.

An up train of empty 100 tonners heads through Barry station behind a 66XXX in September 2007.

A Class 143 Pacer leaves Barry with the 10.05 to Bridgend in October 2016. Mike Back.

The 0942 from Bridgend approaches Barry with a Pacer Unit. Mike Back.

The 0942 from Bridgend to Cardiff Central runs into Barry platform with a Pacer unit. Mike Back.

A diverted HST passes through Palmerston, just east of Cadoxton, with an up service to Paddington on 1 March 1995.

Class 56 56053 with a train of steel coil from Port Talbot Steelworks heads through Palmerston on 1 March 1995.

Class 60 60081 heads through Barry station on a diverted train of coil from Port Talbot Steelworks to the Midlands on 1 March 1995.

A train of covered wagons from Port Talbot Steelworks approaches Barry Station on 21 March 2003.

Class 60 60083 runs through Barry station with a down MGR train to Aberthaw in 2001... with the road clear for the Vale of Glamorgan main line.

A Class 70 diesel 70813 working a train of empties from Aberthaw Power Station round the bend between Gladstone Bridge and Barry Docks station on 2nd November 2017. M.J. Back.

A diverted down HST from Paddington to Swansea passes through Barry on 21 March 2003.

Some steam specials were run via Barry and the Vale in the 1990s as here with 34027 Taw Valley which appears to be going well to tackle the oncoming Porthkerry Bank in this special on 6 April 1996, but came to grief at Bridgend.

A sight I never dreamt I would behold, an A4 at Barry. My final picture for Barry since Dai Woodham and his scrapyard brought such fame to the town, is of the unbelievable sight of 60009 Union of South Africa photographed from Ship Hill Bridge on a lovely sunny morning passing through Barry with a preservation age special en route to Swansea on 21 March 2003.